Mind Matters
Stories for Everyday Mental Wellness

AF094023

OrangeBooks Publication

1st Floor, Rajhans Arcade, Mall Road, Kohka, Bhilai, Chhattisgarh 490020

Website:**www.orangebooks.in**

© Copyright, 2024, Author

All rights reserved. No part of this book may be reproduced, stored in a retrieval system, or transmitted, in any form by any means, electronic, mechanical, magnetic, optical, chemical, manual, photocopying, recording or otherwise, without the prior written consent of its writer.

First Edition, 2024

MIND MATTERS

STORIES FOR EVERYDAY MENTAL WELLNESS

ANITHA NADIG

OrangeBooks Publication
www.orangebooks.in

Dedicated To
*Raghava,
my loving husband
whose unwavering support
has given wings to
my limitless aspirations*

Foreword

All children are the same when they are born except a few, whose development in the mother's womb is impaired because of genetic defect, poor nutritional status of the mother during pregnancy, her ill health and difficult delivery. Every new-born child's brain weighs about 300 grams and contains 10,000 crore nerve cells (Neurons). Though the growth of brains stops at the age of five years after birth, development continues till the age 22 to 25 years. The child has to grow and develop in five areas:

1 Physical

2 Intellectual

3 Emotional

4 Social

5 Ethical

Growth occurs in a step ladder fashion. Each child is different in the growth and development, some are physically strong but weak in intellectual growth. Some are intellectually good but emotionally unstable. Some are introverts and avoid socialisation. Some are very good in social relationships and enjoy interacting with people. Some follow ethical norms, but a few develop criminal and antisocial behaviour. Some may enjoy breaking social, legal and ethical norms, and remain selfish. Some are very good in communication, use language efficiently. All skills are learnt.

Each nerve cell can establish connections with 1000 nerve cells. Many life skills have to be learnt. The speed and overall development of the child depends on many factors, like

1. Genes:

    There are 20,000 genes in every cell carrying the blueprint of development. Genetic makeup of each child is different.

2. Nutrition

3. Parenting and child rearing skills of the parents, personality, emotional makeup and harmony between the parents.

4. Home - Family environment: Type of family - integrated, broken, chaotic, authoritative or democratic family environment.

5. Quality of school, teachers, classmates, quality of education, whether only marks oriented or total personality development. These days, both government and private schools are not children friendly.

6. Media: Gadgets, TV, cinema, internet, are misguiding the children, inducing unhealthy behaviour and addiction.

7. Health problems like nutritional deficiency, obesity, infections, lifestyle, diseases.

8. Social Disparities: Class, caste, religion, language, gender discrimination.

9. Hormones: There are 50 plus hormones in our body which direct and control physical and mental health. Excess or low hormone level leads to ill health and behavioural changes.

10. Neurotransmitters: There are 100 plus neurotransmitters in the brain and nervous system. Dopamine, Serotonin, Oxytocin, Endorphins are wellness neurotransmitters. Love, Affection, Happiness depends on them. Low acetylcholine leads to poor memory. Low dopamine leads to depression. Low serotonin leads to OCD, low GABA leads to anxiety and excess fear.

Mental disorders are divided into major disorders like schizophrenia, bipolar disorder, dementia, addictions. Minor disorders include Depression, Anxiety, Psychosomatic Symptoms, Somatoform disorders.

Medicines, psychotherapy, counselling, making the environment supportive and comfortable, activity and occupational therapies help to treat mental disorders. But in our country, age old beliefs and practices exist. People attribute all mental disorders to God, ghosts, witchcraft, wrong positions of planets, past, bad deeds, bad luck, unknown evil forces. They seek remedy from faith healers.

Severe stigma is attached to mental disorders. They hesitate to consult psychiatrists or psychologists. If they consult, they expect a quick cure and solutions! They ignore academic and behavioural problems of children and adolescents. They label them as lazy, dullards or bad children! They, including teachers, try to punish children.

Many psychiatrists, including me and many psychologists, are trying to educate people through print and electronic media. A recent and welcome book is written by Smt. Anitha Nadig, who is a committed counsellor with vast experience and knowledge. There are 23 chapters starting from 'How much we know about mind and mental health' to 'How to manage emotions, feelings and stress'.

Her language is simple, clear. Her style of presentation is excellent and holds the attention of readers. She gives insight into problems through real case stories. She drives the message straight into the reader's mind, enlightening them with knowledge.

I wish that this book reaches every home to spread the light of mental wellbeing. I expect many more books and write ups from her.

Dr C. R. Chandrashekhar
Former professor of psychiatry
Author & Padmashree awardee

Introduction

Back in the 1990s, as I was entering adolescence, I remember people using 'crazy', 'screw loose', 'psycho', 'mad' very frequently to label people whom they think do not fall under their expectations of 'normal' category. There was a huge stigma around mental illness then. In my teen years, I have seen a person with mental illness locked in a room with hands tied in a chain. None of us then, including the family of that person knew it was mental illness.

Since the last 30 years, I have moved places, changed jobs, and met people from different cultural backgrounds. In my opinion, there is only a slight improvement in not labelling people. The stigma around mental illness is still big in India. Though pandemic brought more awareness about anxiety and depression, more focus on mental health in general in India, neurodivergence, serious mental illness and disorders are still a taboo here.

As per the Global Burden of Disease Study 1990-2017, one in seven Indians were affected by mental disorders in 2017. That means each Indian could have come in close contact with at least one or two people with mental disorders within their family circle, friends, colleagues or in neighbourhood. As per the studies, the top cause for not seeking help for mental illness in India is stigma attached to it.

The statistics of mental disorders in India are alarming and emphasises the need to be aware about mental health and taking timely treatment for it. Mental illness unattended or untreated, is just not a burden to the person having the illness, but to the family and society at large.

In 2012, at the age of 32, I started exploring psychology as a hobby. As I learnt more through books initially and later studying psychology, I was shocked and astonished to understand how the brain plays a major role in human behaviour. I felt, if I had this knowledge, I would have tried not to judge people or not to label people who do not show stereotypical behaviours.

I believe the media is powerful. The writer in me always desired to write about mental illness to bring awareness. It was in my mind but I was waiting for a platform. During the same timelines, my interest in psychology turned into passion. With that I started '**MIND SAKHYA**' in 2020 with a mission '*to help people make friends with their mind*'.

Around this time, I happened to meet Sri. Satyesh N Bellur, an author, speaker and thought leader. He had been offered an Editor-in-Chief position for Vipra Nudi, an English journal. He was looking for a columnist to write about mental health and asked me if I could contribute. Without a second thought, I said YES.

The intention of writing the articles in Vipra Nudi was to educate people on basics of mental health, different types of mental illness, how these disorders can affect a person's life and family. What options are there to seek help? Through these articles, I wanted to bring awareness that mental health is part of overall health. Mental health is also a priority.

In this book, Mind Matters, there are about 23 artefacts written between March 2022 to September 2024. They are in the form of stories, personal experiences and articles. These are not actual case studies but inspired from the real cases. The names used in these stories do not represent any real persons or incidents.

The intent of these stories is to bring awareness about mental health. This should not be taken as a baseline for the diagnosis of an illness or label others with Mental illness. While reading, if you resonate with any symptoms mentioned in these stories and have a doubt, please consult a professional mental health practitioner and get clarity.

The stories in this book are relatable to anyone and everyone. It is also aimed at bringing hope and inspiring people to overcome stigma around mental illness and seek professional help.

I feel my efforts are rewarded if you see any of the below outcomes after reading the book:

- You are moved by the story and can relate with your or someone's life

- You become a little less judgemental and more empathetic with people around you

- You are more aware about mental health and seek support for mental illness

- You educate and encourage others to take treatment for mental health issues

By these outcomes, you would directly or indirectly participate in fighting the mental health stigma.

With that, I sign off now hoping you are reading this book and spreading mental health awareness around you.

Yours warmly
Anitha

Index

1. Mental Health: How Much Do We Know? 1
2. Can You Read My Mind? 5
3. The 'Boy' We Could Not Understand 12
4. Neurodivergence & Academic Performance 22
5. Giving Into Your Obsessions 29
6. Empathy - A Magic Key 35
7. The Cognitive Triangle - Interplay Of Thoughts, Emotions And Behaviors . 39
8. Action Speaks Louder Than Words 43
9. What Does Losing A Job Means To You? 47
10. Management Of Grief 53
11. Suspicious Personality & Relationships 59
12. When There Is A Roadblock On The Memory Lane 66
13. Care For The Caregiver 75
14. Speaking The Right Love Language 83
15. Can Anxiety Influence Your Behaviour? 88
16. How Can The Errors In Thinking Impact Us? 93
17. In The Lap Of Anxiety 105
18. The Scary Pony Ride 111
19. Fight, Flight Or Freeze - Whats Behind This? 118
20. Emotions & Feelings 124

21. Mental Health & Insurance Coverage 131

22. Empowerment Through Emotional Intelligence 136

23. Habit Of Hair Pulling 142

    Acknowledgements 147

    About The Author 150

1
Mental Health: How Much Do We Know?

She was unable to sleep. She was not able to eat. She had lost interest in even the activities which excited her in the past. She was clueless on what was happening to her.

Her husband was also clueless on why she was acting that way. Everything seemed fine to him. He loved her a lot; they had everything they wanted and aspired for - cute kids, a villa, a successful career and a handsome salary. He was unable to understand the cause for her laziness and disinterest in everything, literally everything. He was annoyed with her behaviour. His enquiries on what was bothering her went in vain. She did not tell him the reason. She repeatedly told him she did not know! That annoyed him more and led him to shout at her which was never the case in the past.

She was thinking how her husband had changed. Just a year back, when she had fractured her both legs, the same person so lovingly had taken care of her, in spite of more responsibilities at work and home. Now, he seemed not understanding her at all. He had started shouting at her, which hurt her even more.

After 6 months, a visit to a psychiatrist revealed that she was suffering from depression.

Such scenarios may happen in any of our families. Physical illness is very much visible and hence empathising with the person suffering is easy. Mental illness is INVISIBLE and makes it more complicated to understand what a mentally ill person is going through. It is difficult to comprehend why a person with a poor mental health state acts in a certain way. Hence, it becomes all the more important that we understand mental health better; to ensure we are mentally healthy & help our near and dear one's for a healthy mind.

A healthy body also needs a healthy mind. Mental health is part of overall health. It is as important as physical health.

What Is Mental Health?

As per World Health Organization (WHO) 'Mental health is a state of well-being in which an individual realises his or her own abilities, can cope with the normal stresses of life, can work productively, and is able to make a contribution to his or her family and community'.

Mental health refers to cognitive, intellectual, behavioural and emotional wellbeing. It is about how people think, feel and act. Mental health can affect our daily living, relationships, work and physical health.

Why Is Mental Health Important?

Almost all the activities we do in a state of wakefulness involves thinking, feeling and acting. Any impairment in thinking, emotions or behaviour can impact life in multiple ways. It can affect different aspects of our life -it could be productivity and focus at office, quality of our relationships, self-image, managing stress, how to reach our goals and so on. As we have started understanding mental health, there may be various questions arising in your mind.

What Is Mental Illness?

Knowing about mental illness helps in recognizing it as well as overcoming the stigma of mental illness. Mental illness is a health condition which affects emotions, thinking and behaviours or combination of these. It creates distress and problems dealing with relationships, work or any social activities. Mental illness is also referred to as Mental disorders. Some people may have mental illness, while few may temporarily go through poor mental health in certain circumstances. People with severe mental disorders may have illusions, wrong beliefs and neglect their needs.

Causes Of Mental Illness

Many people who are diagnosed with mental illness have this question, 'Why me?'. What is the cause of getting a mental illness?

Mental illness cannot be attributed to a single cause. Usually, it is a combination of biological, psychological and environmental factors.

Biological: There are many reasons for physical illness; it could be an infection, hormonal imbalance or an injury to name a few. Sometimes it could be even hereditary. Likewise, mental illness can also occur due to infection or chemical imbalance in the brain or brain injury, substance abuse and so on.

Psychological: Any abuse (physical, emotional or sexual) in childhood leads to a psychological trauma and hence may be a cause of mental illness. Neglect of the child or loss of a parent can also cause mental illness.

Environmental: Death or divorce, changing schools or places, social or cultural pressures or negative life events, financial problems can contribute to mental illness.

When we are physically ill, we initially may do a home remedy, if that doesn't help, reach out to a doctor to get professional help. Certain illnesses may need hospitalisation or long-term treatments. Similarly, mental illness also needs professional help. It may call for short term or long-term treatment and/or therapies. A very few cases may need hospitalisation or rehabilitation.

Do you want to know more about mental health? Mental illness and stigma around them? What exactly are these illnesses? How can one identify mental illness or poor mental health? Whom to reach out to? Reading books and articles or videos in social media from **reliable sources** can help you.

2

Can You Read My Mind?

We were visiting my aunt in Shivamogga last week. Citing reasons for visiting our family god temple, we decided to visit my father's ancestral place which is about an hour's drive from Shivamogga. After a joyful drive in the rain due to the cyclone effect in Andhra, we reached this place in an hour. After the pooja rituals, we started visiting some of my dad's cousins who live there.

We went to meet one of my dad's cousins and his family. He was pleasantly surprised by our visit and welcomed us with a lot of excitement. After the initial exchange of greetings, my dad introduced me to his cousin. I did a namaste and smiled at him and said 'Nice to meet you uncle'. With a smile on his face, he said 'Nice to meet you too. We usually do not get to meet our cousin's children. I am glad you came'. I smiled and nodded not knowing how to respond. After enquiring about where I live, 'Do you work?' he asked. 'Yes uncle. I am a Counselling Psychologist. I have my own practice in Bangalore', I took out my business card and handed it over to him.

'Oh! Psychologist? So, you can read people's minds, right?' he blurted out with a curiosity in his voice. I smiled and paused. Curiosity in his voice told me from my experience what was coming next.

'Can you tell me what is in my mind now?' he said with a mischievous smile on his face. To his disappointment, I said 'No uncle. I cannot read others minds.

'Really?', his voice dropped as if my response seemed to disappoint him.

'But you are trained to say whether a person is good or bad by talking to them, right?'

Being used to such questions, I took a deep breath to explain a bit. 'Uncle, that is the usual understanding people have about psychologists or counsellors. We are trained and taught not to judge our clients. That is part of our ethics. Categorising a person as good or bad is more of a judgement. We only care about our client's concerns and what is the reason they have come for counselling and how to help them to get better'. As I finished, I noticed another elderly woman and a young lady had already joined the conversation and were listening.

Uncle introduced them as his wife and daughter. After the exchange of greetings, the uncle told his wife that I am a psychologist. She asked, 'You mean you are a mind doctor?'. I could not control my smile on hearing the word 'mind doctor'. I said, 'yes & no' with a half-smile.

Looking at her puzzled face, I continued, 'I work with human minds. But I am not a doctor'. I paused and observed the confused faces around me. 'Both psychologists and psychiatrists work with human minds. Psychiatrist is a medical doctor specialised in the human mind. They are the people who has bachelor's degree in medicine, i.e., MBBS and then masters in psychiatry, like other specialisations after MBBS – Orthopaedic, cardiology and so on. They are the people who can decide whether a medicine should be given to a person with mental illness or disorder. They assess the illness or mental disturbance based on clinical symptoms. Psychologists on the other hand, are professionally qualified people who assess, diagnose and treat emotional, thought related and behavioural problems through counselling. Counselling is also called 'Talk Therapy'. I took out the water bottle from my bag to take a sip of water.

Uncle's daughter hesitantly asked me, 'I am entering second year of Pre-University. I have taken 'psychology' as an elective. Can I ask you a few questions?'.

I was delighted to hear that she has opted for an elective as psychology. My energy levels doubled to talk more about psychology. To confirm her name which I saw on the certificates on walls, I asked, 'Kavya right?'. She nodded with a smile. 'Please go-ahead Kavya. I am happy to share whatever I know and have learnt'.

With a curious tone she asked, 'I want to know what is counselling and what exactly happens in counselling'. 'That is a very good question Kavya', I said. Before I continued, her father interrupted, 'I have heard that counselling means giving advice, isn't it? People have various problems and they do not know how to solve them. When they go to a counsellor, the counsellor solves their problems by giving advice. Am I right?', he turned to me, awaiting my response.

'Good you brought this point', I was happy he asked this question. I continued with enthusiasm. 'It is a misconception people have that counselling means advice giving. But it is not true. Counsellor neither gives advice nor any ready-made solutions to client's problems.

'Then how does the counsellor help in solving others' problems?', uncle's wife asked.

'Counselling is a process of listening to the clients' problems, bringing awareness about what they are going through, what is bothering them and helping them find a solution on their own. In this process, clients are helped to identify the emotions generated from the problem, what kinds of thoughts are going in their mind, how they behave in such situations and what physical symptoms trouble them. As part of the treatment, counsellors also teach techniques to the clients to deal with their thoughts, behaviours and emotions constructively. If the counsellor feels that the problem is deeper and any symptoms of mental disorder, they will refer the client to either clinical psychologists who do the diagnosis or the psychiatrists for medicines.

Kavya seemed to reflect upon what I said and asked, 'That is why counselling is called talk therapy. You don't give any medicines but talk to the client, teach some skills to deal with their problems'.

'Absolutely' I said, amazed by her inference.

'What kind of problems do people usually bring in for counselling?' Aunty asked, shifting her sitting position.

'People come for counselling with various kinds of problems. Any emotional or behavioural issues, negative thinking, over thinking, work stress, relationship issues, coping with long term physical illness, grief due to any loss, anxiety, depression and so on. Some people recognize these problems are hampering their peace of mind, happiness or productivity and performance in their day today life and seek counselling. Some are not aware that counselling can help them to deal or accept issues bothering them in their life' I paused. Aunty looked eager to ask a question. She removed her spectacles and said, 'Their problems seem to be very personal. How can one discuss their personal issues with a counsellor? How safe is it?'

'Yes Aunty. Everyone who approaches for counselling will have this concern. Many people do not seek counselling because they are not sure whatever they discuss will be kept confidential. Counsellors are taught and trained to keep confidentiality. Whatever is discussed in the session is not shared to anybody. But except if the counsellor sees a self-harming tendency of the client, the counsellor is bound to inform the family for safety reasons. In such cases as well, only clients' symptoms of self-harm are shared and instructions for client's safety with family and not any other contents discussed. Counsellor may discuss client's case with a supervisor for supervision without disclosing the client's identity'.

'Just one last question', Kavya said. 'What is the difference between a counsellor and a psychologist?'.

'There are different terminologies used. Counsellors usually deal with milder forms of mental health issues. They could be trained professionals with or without a master's degree in psychology. Counselling Psychologists have a master's degree in psychology and deal with moderate to serious mental health issues. There is another category called clinical psychologists. They either have a doctorate degree (PhD) or MPhil and assess and diagnose mental illness and disorders along with counselling & therapies. They often work in medical setups and hospitals. Psychotherapists, are psychologists with specialisation in specific areas like family therapy, marital therapy, anxiety and so on'.

Aunty came from the kitchen holding glasses filled with juice on a tray. Uncle asked, 'I am wondering, does counselling really help people to solve their problems?'.

I smiled and said, 'Beautiful question uncle. Counselling is something like attending a driving class. Do you learn driving after attending a driving class?'.

He laughed loudly. 'My two sons attended driving classes last year. One of them learnt it well but the other one is still struggling'. Aunty added to his statement, 'My younger son, after the driving course, used to take his uncles and friends' car and practised. So, he became good at driving. My elder son hardly makes an attempt to drive. We can't blame him also, as we do not have a car', her voice dropped towards the end.

'You called that point out very well aunty. What I wanted to convey was, in a counselling engagement, a client's interest and effort is very important to bring the best results. Willingness and motivation from the client are required to practise and apply the learnings from the counselling session on one hand and on the other hand a supportive ecosystem also helps to make progress'.

'It was an insightful conversation today' uncle said, finishing the juice.

'You people have a curious mind and interest to know about this stigmatic topic. I really appreciate you all for initiating this conversation' I said, keeping the glass on the teapoy. I turned to Aunty and said, 'The juice was really tasty. It had been a long time since I drank bitter lemon juice. I thanked her for the home-grown bitter lemon juice. Aunty and Kavya went to prepare the food for us and we went with uncle to see the big areca nut garden behind the house.

3
The 'Boy' We Could Not Understand

Ashwathi sat there restlessly while her husband Hemanth drove the car. She could hear her heart beating. It was beating little faster than the usual, her palms were sweaty. She was very anxious about attending the parent-teacher meeting. She was thinking what will the teacher say this time about her son, Aarav. He is 5 and half years old and is in UKG. The last three Parent - Teacher meetings had been increasingly stressful for her. Last two years were not so stressful. Aarav, when he was enrolled to nursery at the age of three and a half was only speaking very few two and three letter words. Kids of his age in her community had started making sentences. On comparing with kids of his age, Ashwathi felt he was way behind his speech. Hemanth and his parents were not as worried about Ashwathi as Hemanth also started speaking later than his age kids. When they went to enrol Aarav for school, the principal quickly noticed his speech delay and gave a lot of assurance that he would learn and be able to speak like others. She also told that every kid has its own learning pace and they would give an extra care for him and review every quarter.

Her thoughts came to a halt when the car suddenly stopped. Hemanth was shouting at a two-wheeler guy in front, scolding him of not knowing how to ride a bike. Ashwathi noticed that Hemanth face was tensed and fists tight. She knows that his anger is more to do with Aarav's behaviours and feedback and complaints they were getting from the school and fellow parents rather than on the two-wheeler guy. Hemanth and two-wheeler guy were arguing on whose mistake it was though there was no visible damage to any of the vehicles. She didn't want to interfere in that fight as she knew his anger would turn on her. As the traffic cop came, their argument ended and vehicles started moving again.

She started reflecting on how their relationship had changed in last three years. First three years after Aarav was born was so beautiful. Hemanth used to spend a lot of time with Aarav every day. He used to feed him in the night, play with him and ensured she gets enough rest herself as she was also working. They were a happy family. Things started changing after that. Aarav was growing and he had lot of energy. As he learnt walking, he started walking around, running, jumping, pulling things off like any other kid. Hemanth parents who used to take care of their grandson along with a nanny could not match up to Aarav's energy level. Frequent change of nanny's led to Aarav's tantrums and meltdowns. Ashwathi started missing office, frequent work from home and her work used to get piled up. It was difficult for her to juggle between the tasks. Hemanth kept saying once he starts going to school, it would be better.

The hope of things getting better after enrolling Aarav to school went in vain. They started seeing different challenges. Aarav, as he was not able to speak at the level of others kids, other kids started facing difficulties communicating with him. Most of the times, it led to fights between the kids. Aarav hitting or kicking other kids. Aarav was strong physically comparing with kids of his age. Once it happened, he had pushed a kid and the kid fell down and hurt his forehead badly by hitting to the corner of a table having a cut in the forehead. The kids' parents became furious and anxious and complained. Aarav's parents had to meet the other kid's parents and apologise. School people asked Aarav's parents to spend more time with Aarav. They said, Aarav may be having an emotional issue which is coming out as behavioural issue. Similar incidents started happening in their community in the evenings when Aarav was taken out to play by nanny. Nanny's kept quitting. Ashwathi and Hemanth discussed and decided that Ashwathi to quit the job to take care of Aarav and give him more attention.

Things didn't get better. Rather, Ashwathi started seeing more and more of Aarav's different behaviour patterns. His speech had improved. But Aarav was not responding to the call of his name by others. He was not making eye contact while talking. He used to tease other kids repeatedly. He used to constant jump and run around. He got into fights quickly and showed meltdowns when he did not get what he wants or the way he wanted it. She heard people calling him, 'very naughty', 'hyper kid', 'aggressive kid' and so on. It hurt her a lot. When she shared her feelings and observations with

Hemanth, he used to dismiss her feelings. He used to say, 'you are over thinking'. But Hemanth started feeling the pressure when Aarav's teacher started telling them to see a counsellor. They went to principal to discuss it. She mentioned that Aarav seems to have a challenge with social skills and communication. It is beyond their capacity to help Aarav to learn these skills. She gave them the details of the counsellor they could meet.

Hemanth was so angry; he had gotten into an argument with the principal. He was very angry for two-three days. He kept saying that the school was not good and he would put Aarav in a different school, teachers are not well trained and so on. In the next PTM, principal followed up with them on meeting the counsellor. When she heard no progress on that, she also subtlety mentioned that either they need to meet a counsellor and take help or they may have to change their school as they are not trained enough to handle Aarav. Again, Hemanth had become angry. He blamed Ashwathi for not parenting Aarav well. Ashwathi, already who was going through lot of guilt and self-doubt on her parenting started feeling worse. The relationship between husband and wife was slowly drifting apart and had strained over the two years.

Ashwathi came to present on hearing a loud honking from Hemanth. They had reached the school gate. They parked their car and hesitantly went inside the school. There were other parents waiting for their turns. They sat there waiting to be called. A staff member came and told them that they were running late and it would take 15 minutes for their turn.

Hemanth opened his laptop and started working while they sat there waiting. Ashwathi strolled into the area where classes were conducted. As she was walking in the corridor, she heard a loud cry and immediately recognised that it was her son Aarav crying. She was not sure if she should go into the class. She knew if he sees her, what would happen for next one hour. She would not be able to attend the PTM. With tears in her eyes and heaviness in her heart, she came back to the waiting room. Hemanth, raised his eyebrows looking at her. She just turned away, wiping her tears.

Their turn came and they hesitantly walked in. To their surprise they saw three people sitting there. Aarav's teacher, principal and one more person they had never seen before. After initial greetings, they introduced Shyamala, a 40-year-old lady as a counsellor. Principal told them that 'As we had informed earlier, we are experimenting with having a counsellor visit the school for 2 days a week. This would help us to understand the children better and also extend the services for parents on parenting, child developmental milestones and dealing with kids emotional and behavioural issues.

A little taken aback, Hemanth didn't know how to respond; Ashwathi smiled and greeted the counsellor. Principal looked at the counsellor and nodded and started talking. 'Mr and Mrs Hemanth, you must have seen our messages on the dairy and WhatsApp that we conducted few activities for kids last month. We did singing, dancing, running, painting activities, memory games and so on. We want to show you few videos of Aarav participating in that'.

Both Ashwathi and Hemanth forgot their anxiety and anger for the moment and curiously waited to watch the videos. They showed the first video where a group of children dancing to the latest Bollywood song. While most of the children did a repeated steps and seemed average in dancing, Aarav seemed dancing very well, showing different steps. He also did quick jumps and somersaults rhythmically aligning to the music. A smile and proudness emerged on Ashwathi & Hemanth's face for the first time after a long time. Ashwathi, enthusiastically said, 'I knew he likes dance. But as we live in the apartment, I can't let him dance as much because of the complaints from the people living in the below floor. He seems to be enjoying the dance well'. Hemanth took it from there, 'Wow, this is awesome. I have seen only his tantrums more and never knew the other side of him'.

Principal smiled and said we have more. They showed a video of a running race. Aarav was way too forward than other children in running. Hemanth and Ashwathi were smiling again. There were tears rolling down from Ashwathi's eyes. Shyama, the counsellor, notices the parents' emotions, 'Do you see your son's strengths?'. They nodded in silence.

The Counsellor continued, 'Every child is unique. Each kid has his own pace of learning and development. As a parent and teacher, we need to understand this and help the child in their learning and development' She paused. 'But madam, what do you do when the kids learning is way too behind the other kids of the same age? For example, Aarav's speech is not on par with his age. Forget about his age children, it is not on par with kids younger to him'. Sensing the anxiety in Ashwathi's tone, the counsellor says, 'Indeed as a parent, one gets worried in such cases. The best thing to do is to consult a child counsellor. There are developmental milestones for kids. As a layman we are not experts to say whether it is really a delay, a cause for concern or whether we can wait and watch. A child counsellor is professionally qualified and can guide and direct on what to do in such cases.

'So, in our case madam, I am not sure if you have met Aarav. What should we do? Principal madam had told us to meet a counsellor. But we really are worried what if our kid is labelled as a 'mental' person', Hemanth shares his fear.

The Counsellor nods, 'Yes Mr. Hemanth. This fear is very common in all of us. Unfortunately, mental health is not considered as part of overall health and there is a stigma and that leads not to take help. Let me ask you a question.

Have you seen people with 6 fingers? people who use their left hand dominantly? or someone who was born blind?'

Hemanth and Ashwathi nod their heads indicating they have seen such people.

The Counsellor asks, 'What do you think of them? Why are they like that?'

Before Ashwathi opens her mouth, Hemanth, 'Not everyone is the same madam? There are certain conditions people get by birth. Maybe it is genetic or something to do with the pregnancy'.

Ashwathi adds, 'My niece has squinted eyes, madam. But we need to accept that. My sister is very sad and worried about it. I tell her not to comment on this and treat her like a normal child. It should not generate a low self confidence in her right?'

'You guys are so well aware and understanding', the counsellor pauses.

Ashwathi, 'Madam, can you please guide us on Aarav?'

There are exceptional abilities found in some of the people with Autism, ADHD and LD. For example, Albert Einstein had Dyslexia, a learning disorder. Abhishek Bacchan has dyslexia too. Britney Spears, an American songwriter and actress, has ADHD. The famous Charles Darwin had autism. So, people with these neurological conditions can be intelligent, lead a normal life and be successful in life too. We as parents and teachers need to identify their strengths, help them in the learning journey and deal with their limitations. The way of teaching for the kids with these conditions may be different, based on the severity levels' '.

The Counsellor stops to drink water. Hemanth, 'What should be our next step?'.

'I observed Aarav last week and had few interactions with him. I see a challenge in social skills and communications mainly. It is better to get it diagnosed by a developmental psychologist'.

Ashwathi in an anxious voice, 'What is your diagnosis madam?'

'I am a counsellor. Only a developmental psychologist can help with diagnosis. As a child counsellor, I see an indication of one of these conditions. But it is better to get it diagnosed rather than speculating.'

Ashwathi, 'Whom do we contact for diagnosis?'

'I will share with you the details of the counselling centre and the developmental psychologist. You can take an appointment. They will give multiple activities and tasks for Aarav and ask you to take up a few questionnaires. Based on those results, they give the diagnosis. It will take about 2-3 hours, 'the counsellor takes out a card from her bag and gives it to Ashwathi.

Both their energy levels shifted showing some hope. They thank the counsellor, teacher and the principal before coming out of the meeting room. A staff member says that Aarav is waiting outside his class to be picked up. As Hemanth walks into the corridor of the classrooms, he sees Aarav doing multiple somersaults on the grass in front of the classroom. A smile crossed his face indicating happiness.

They came back home. Both of them feeling mixed emotions, Hemanth decides to take off from work for the rest of the day. He makes a coffee for himself and picks the newspaper to read. An article on the 5th page catches his attention with a title **'Is Autism a**

disability or a neuro divergence condition? with a subtitle 02-April: World Autism Awareness Day. He reads through the article while mentally connecting the dots. He gives the newspaper to Ashwathi, 'Read this article. Where is that card? I will book an appointment with the psychologist for this week'.

4
Neurodivergence & Academic Performance

There is a well-known saying that 'Teachers can open the door, but you must enter it yourself'. With more research into neurodiversity*, it is discovered that not everyone's brain is developed the same way. It is very similar to us not having exactly the same eyes as our siblings, the same nose as our dad's or the same ability to run like that of an athlete. But we are all unique in our own ways and have our own strengths.

'Rakshith is thirteen years old and is studying in 8th grade. He is very active and social in school and his neighbourhood. He is labelled as a talkative boy in his surroundings. After his mid-term exams, his parents were called for a parent - teachers meeting. Rakhsith has got very low grades in maths and average in other subjects. Both teachers and parents concluded that the covid times had hit him badly and lost some learning on maths due to online classes. Also, his talkative nature is distracting him from studies and being strict and getting a tutor should help him in improving his learning.'

'Srishti and Drishti are eleven years old and twins. Both of them put their parents on task by being very naughty. Getting them ready, making them do their homework is a mammoth task for their parents. They dread school holidays as it gets them exhausted. Both Srishti and Drishti have a resistance to writing. Both parents and teachers attribute it towards their naughtiness. They say that they don't sit and focus on writing because they are always distracted with one or other things. Srishti takes a longer time to finish her homework if her mother sits with her and assists. But it is very difficult for the parents to make Drishti complete even half of her homework. This issue reflects in exams too.'

It is a common challenge for most parents to get their kids to focus on studies, make them finish their homework and ensure they give their best effort for the exams. We may think that the kids are either lazy or not being serious and hence the poor or average academic results. While this can be a possibility, the way the kids' brain is developed or wired may not support them to learn certain subjects on par with other kids.

As per a study, about 1 in 5 to 6 children are neurodivergent. **The variations in brain development in neurodivergent kids leads to conditions like Learning Disorder, Autism and Attention Deficit and Hyperactive Disorder.**

'After a year, even with Rakshith's parents assisting him in his studies and homework and getting a home tutor for maths, there was a very slight improvement in his performance in maths but not significant. His parents became anxious and alert as he was about to enter 10th grade, which has a board exam. School authorities suggested that they take professional help and hence they consulted a counsellor.'

'Srishti and Drishti's mother happened to attend a neurodiversity session from her office which led her to think about her daughter's writing challenge. She discussed it with her husband and they decided to consult a psychologist to rule out any learning disorder with their daughters.'

A recent study in the US states that there are 4 million kids with Learning Disabilities (LD) in the USA. 18% of them dropout of school or college due to lack of intervention at the early stage. Good news is that LD can be diagnosed at an early stage. There are special educators outside school for kids with LD to support them in their learning. In India it is estimated that 10% of children have LD.

'Rakshith's parents met a counsellor who guided them to a clinical psychologist to get a psychometric test done to rule out LD. The test confirmed that Rakshith had Dyscalculia, a type of LD where the brain does not support learning maths. Their psychologist also briefed and counselled the parents about an option to drop maths as a subject and take an alternate subject where Rakshith has an ability to learn. This information reduced Rakshith's parents' worries a bit.'

'Srishti and Drishti's parents consulted a clinical psychologist and briefed her about their daughter's challenge with writing. The psychologist gave a psychometric test for both the kids. The result showed that Srishti had moderate challenges in writing while Drishti had severe challenges in writing, that is Dysgraphia (an inability or difficulty to write due to a neurological condition). Good part was that both didn't have any issues with reading or comprehending and understanding the subjects. Psychologists advised parents to talk to the school to seek support to enable the kids in their writing. She also mentioned that the government has rules that school should provide a scribe for the exam (a person to write while the kid with dysgraphia states the answers in the exam) or give extra time for the kid to write.'

Government has come up with policies to enable and support children with learning disabilities. According to this policy, education boards should accommodate and enable kids with learning disabilities with their learning journey. Exemptions and opting for a scribe or a reader involves a process, which may differ in each education board. Disability Certificate is issued by the Disability Committee of any district hospital in our state.

'Rakshith's parents produced a LD certificate to the school and requested for change in subject. School authorities contacted the board and provided alternate subject options. Rakshith selected environmental science instead of maths.'

'The board suggested the school give extra time for Srishthi in exams while for Drishti, a scribe was given in exams.'

Here is an example of relaxation from an educational board for reference. It may vary slightly from board to board. Many schools may not be aware of these relaxations and parents may have to request and insist school authorities to enquire and enable the students with LD.

1. 'Scribe for writing' or 'extra time for writing' to students with writing issues (Dyscalculia). The board or the examination centre usually provides the scribe but parents can also apply for the scribe. Remuneration for the scribe may be given by the board.

2. Students with reading disabilities(dyslexia) can opt for a reader. A reader is a person who just reads and does not explain.

3. If the kid has difficulties with languages, the board offers one compulsory language as against two. Students can opt for another subject with options provided by the board and drop one language.

LD comes with different severity. Based on the psychometric test results, clinical psychologist suggests, if the kid needs a relaxation or a special educator.

Process involved to opt for the relaxations may include but not limited to these steps.

1. Psychometric test for the student to assess the LD. This has to be done by a RCI licensed clinical psychologist. Clinical psychologists provide a certificate which is accepted by the

board or the government. In every district, a district surgeon is authorised to issue the disability certificate.

2. Usually, schools may suggest some counselling centres or hospitals from where they accept the certificate. If the school does not have this reference, one may go to a clinical psychologist with a RCI licence or who works in the department of psychiatry of a district hospital.

3. Parents need to submit this certificate to school authorities. School authorities will in turn submit this to the board and get an approval.

4. In some boards, it may be required to get a signature of a government authority from the education department. School should be able to help the parents with the process.

5. The whole process may take from 3-6 months. It is better if the parent starts the process as early as in the end of the 8th grade or beginning of the 9th grade to finish the process before 10th grade starts. This avoids the stress and burden for both the parent and the kid when the kid enters the academic year for the board exam.

There are kids with learning disabilities with above average intelligence. LD does not mean low intelligence. It just means that the kid has different strengths. Parents can explore the strengths of the kid and enable their learning journey and career in their strength areas. Taking a career aptitude test in 8th grade or 9th grade gives enough time for kids and parents to understand the natural abilities of the kid and plan their next course of action for the kid's further studies.

Marks and academic performance increase the opportunities for further studies and career opportunities. But life skills help the kid to tread through life's problems and have a happy and successful life.

Neurodiversity is the term used to describe differences in the way people's brains work. It emphasises that there is no right or wrong in the way the brain works. It is just that one brain can be different from the other and hence the capabilities of an individual. Neurodiversity is more used in the context of Autism, Attention Deficit Hyperactivity Disorder (ADHD) and Learning Disorders. Though these were termed as disorders or viewed as deficits earlier, recent studies have termed it as differences in the brain rather than deficit or a disability.

5
Giving Into Your Obsessions

'Raksha and Bharath were worried about their daughter Sanvi. For three months, Sanvi was consistently late to school. She used to miss the prayers regularly. Punishments and warnings didn't seem to bring any change in her behaviour. Raksha and Bharath's effort to help her get ready also didn't help much. The school authorities have asked Sanvi to meet the school counsellor.'

'Nishanth is a software developer, who got recruited by a Singapore based company. He is very brilliant and of adobe normal intelligence. He has been working for three years and he has not received any promotions while his peers have moved up one step in their career ladder. He is getting the same feedback in his performance review every year. The complaint about him is he is neither on time to office nor to any of the meetings, even the client meetings. This time, his manager asked him to meet a psychologist.'

'Jaya is a school teacher and has hopped three to four schools in the last six years. She has lost her jobs in the schools for the same reason - coming late to school. Seeing the same challenges faced by Jaya, her husband advised her to meet a therapist.'

Over the years and months, Sanvi, Nishanth and Jaya have realised that they are unable to come out of this habit in spite of making efforts. They are frustrated with this behaviour but do not know how to come out of it. Finally, they decided to seek professional help.

On meeting the counsellor, they were diagnosed with OCD - obsessive compulsive disorder.

Obsessive-Compulsive Disorder (OCD):

The American Psychiatric Association defines OCD as a disorder in which people have recurring, unwanted thoughts, ideas or sensations (obsessions). To get rid of the thoughts, they feel driven to do something repetitively (compulsions). The repetitive behaviours, such as hand washing/cleaning, checking on things, and mental acts like (counting) or other activities, can significantly interfere with a person's daily activities and social interactions.

Obsessions:

Obsessions bring fear, anxiety or disgust. They are shown in the form of recurrent and persistent thoughts, impulses or images. People with OCD recognize that these obsessions are not rational. The intrusive thoughts are so excessive and unreasonable that even thinking logically does not help to stop the compulsions. People with OCD, ease the distress either by compulsive behaviours or distract themselves with other activities.

Compulsions:

Compulsions are repetitive behaviours (washing hands multiple times) in response to obsession. This compulsive behaviour can also be a mental act like rumination, mental rehearsals and counting. In the severe cases of OCD, compulsions affect the daily activities and routine badly.

'Rakhsa and Bharath took Sanvi to the counsellor. They explained how Sanvi takes more time in getting ready for school. On probing her, the counsellor discovered that Sanvi feels clean only after using twenty mugs of water. She feels that germs in her teeth get cleaned only after brushing teeth for four rounds. If she does not stick to these specific numbers, it causes her distress. To avoid the distress, she sticks to those numbers.'

'Nishanth already had an awareness that his time management issue was something to do with his mental health. With his research skills, he had already read many articles about OCD and had suspected that he may have OCD. But he needed a push to seek professional help.

When he met the psychologist. He explained his problems well without probing. He mentioned that he is a religious person and does pooja every day. He feels something bad will happen if pooja is missed. Also, his bowel does not get cleared at once in the morning. He feels that his bowel gets cleared only after going to the toilet three times. He also carries this belief that if he goes to the toilet after taking bath and before doing pooja, he should take bath again to do pooja. If he thinks to skip any of these self-inflicted rules, he gets scared that something bad will happen. To overcome the fear, he ends up doing all these compulsions and then leaves for the office.'

'Jaya met the therapist along with her husband. During the discussion, Jaya's husband shared his observations about Jaya's compulsive behaviour of rechecking the stove, geyser and locks before leaving home and her obsession with keeping things in a symmetry.

On further probing Jaya, she confessed that she has the habit of rechecking twice whether the geyser and stove have been switched off. Once she locks the door and takes the lift, she starts doubting if the door is locked and again comes back to recheck. If she does not recheck, she starts thinking about the catastrophic effects of a house being robbed or burned down. To avoid those thoughts, she rechecks again and again before leaving for school.

She also spends a good amount of time keeping the kids and her husband's slippers in order in the shoe rack before leaving. All these activities take time and Jaya ends up late in school.'

OCD Can Be Broadly Categorised Into 5 Types:

1. Contamination obsessions with cleaning compulsions
2. Symmetry obsessions with ordering compulsions
3. Harm obsessions with checking compulsions
4. Obsessions without visible compulsions

5. Hoarding Compulsions

Sanvi was diagnosed with contamination obsession and cleaning compulsion whereas Nishanth's case was of harm obsessions with checking compulsions. Jaya had both harm obsessions and checking compulsion as well as symmetry obsessions and ordering compulsion.

They were psycho educated about OCD and its types. An awareness was brought about how it is affecting their daily routine and goals. They were briefed about the therapy approach and duration.

All three of them are undergoing Cognitive Behavioural Therapy (CBT), Exposure and Response Prevention (ERP) therapy for OCD. Mindfulness techniques are also being taught to them to deal with their fear and anxieties.

CBT helps in identifying the unhelpful ways of thinking (Cognitive distortions) and unhelpful behaviour patterns. It teaches techniques on how to deal with unhelpful thoughts and behaviours and to change them. Counselling with CBT includes problem solving and healthier ways of coping with difficult situations.

ERP helps people to reduce their anxiety by slowly exposing them to the perceived threatening situations in a controlled environment. It also encourages people to prevent compulsive behaviour. ERP is not about eliminating the anxiety but accepting and learning to manage it.

Medicines which increase the availability of Serotonin Neurotransmitters in the brain are prescribed by psychiatrists which should be given for a long time. These medicines are safe and have no severe side effects.

Research is still going on to find the exact cause of the OCD. There are various theories about OCD where experts say that OCD occurrence can have multiple factors contributing. Some of them include genetic, neurological, behavioural, cognitive and the environment.

Avoiding the occurrence of OCD is not in our hands. But understanding it and learning to deal with it is absolutely in our hands.

6
Empathy - A Magic Key

Often, we may hear this statement from people around us or we may make this statement - 'He does not understand' / 'People don't understand my situation' / I don't feel understood by him'. Along with these thoughts, a range of emotions - hurt, anger, sadness, betrayal and so on may stem. What is missing in a conversation which leads people not being understood? When & how will you feel understood in a conversation? What exactly makes you feel understood by your loved one's or even your boss?

It is difficult to comprehend and answer these questions. Isn't it? At least, for me initially it was.

Cambridge dictionary defines 'empathy' as 'the ability to share someone else's feelings or experiences by imagining what it would be like to be in that person's situation'.

Empathy is the ability to understand how one feels, experiences things from their point of view and feeling what they are feeling.

Empathy means imagining yourself going through the same situation as that of the other and feeling the suffering in the same way. For example, if your friend has lost a loved one, imagining you have lost a loved one and going through that emotionally.

One of the issues frequently seen in couple and child counselling or counselling for work stress is that people complain of not being understood by their significant other.

Azgar, a 14-year-old boy, opened up to counsellor in one of the sessions discussing his anger towards his parents like this - 'My parents do not understand me'. On probing, he mentioned a recent incident of falling sick with food poisoning and how he was treated by his parents. Despite his parents taking him to the doctor, starting medicines at the earliest and attending to him day and night, he felt not being understood. But he felt understood by his grandmother, who lived far away from him. What is the difference? While his parents kept telling him repeatedly that he fell sick because he ate outside. In Spite of telling him not to eat outside, he does this repeatedly. But his grandmother called him twice a day, asking him 'how is his stomach pain?', 'how is he feeling now?', 'was he able to sleep enough?'.

31-year-old Drishti, complains about his husband in a couple session. She says that her husband does not allow her to speak completely. He won't listen to what she wants to say.

Zara, who is 40 years old and a director in a company, says that it is becoming very difficult to deal with her boss. Every conversation is draining her and creating stress. She feels that her boss is not understanding her situation and challenges. He thinks of his times, how things were run. He does not see that times have changed, people have changed.

Some people seem to be naturally empathetic in nature. Others may feel it difficult to show their empathy. There are various reasons why a person may not be empathetic. But, when we look at empathy as a skill to build, here are a few tips on how one can build empathy.

Listening: Listening is an important part of empathy. Listening to understand rather than to respond is very important. When people are upset and sharing their thoughts, you can show gestures of nodding, occasionally making eye contact and using words like 'okay', 'I got it' and so on.

Give a pause when they stop talking. They may not have completed what they want to share. Listening without interrupting is another aspect of listening. Be mindful about your body language while listening.

Paraphrasing: Paraphrasing means repeating what you have understood. You can start sentences with phrases like 'I see that…', 'I sense that.' or 'I hear you'. Paraphrasing helps a person to feel understood and also sometimes helps to reflect upon their feelings. This may also encourage them to talk more. Be mindful about your tone while talking.

Putting Yourself In Their Shoes: Think about their situation by putting yourself in their shoes. How you might have felt, how you might have reacted. Process that before you respond to them.

Check On Their Feelings: Ask them open ended questions like 'how are you feeling now?', 'How are you dealing with it? 'What's running in your mind?'. This helps them to acknowledge their feelings and thoughts. It also helps to reflect upon them.

Offer Support: Before closing the conversation, offer them help. You can just ask 'How can I help you?' or can be more specific - 'You can tell me when you feel like talking.' or offer any help that you feel you can do. Check on them how they are doing as a follow up.

Empathy does not mean you need to agree to whatever they are saying. You understand their point of view but you can communicate that you have a different opinion.

Being empathetic makes people understood. When people are understood, it strengthens the relationship. Empathy is one of the keys to your personal and professional success.

7

The Cognitive Triangle - Interplay Of Thoughts, Emotions And Behaviors

We humans are not consistent in our behaviours. If you have paid attention to human behaviour, you might have noticed that different people behave/react/respond differently to the same situation. A person may react to similar situations differently, in different timelines or with different people.

A boss may yell at his team member for missing an important delivery. Another person in the same position and same situation may give critical feedback without yelling and get the work done.

A mother-in-law may feel very happy that her son-in-law helps her daughter in the kitchen. Same person may get annoyed when his son helps her daughter-in-law in the kitchen.

We might have noticed such a change in behaviours within us as well.

Ever wondered what may be the reason?

Reasons for human behaviour is a very vast and deep topic. While there are numerous reasons why a person's nature or behaviour is in a certain way, in this article we will focus on learning about the cognitive triangle, the interplay of thoughts, emotions and behaviours.

Assume you are walking on a street. Suddenly, you see a snake close to your path. What happens to you? You get scared. You may get thoughts like - 'Oh my god. Snake! It could be poisonous. What if it bites me?'. Then you ensure you go away from the snake. Call up a snake catcher if it is in your office or apartment premise. Alert others about the snake.

You see a snake as you walk along a street. You get scared for a moment. Then, when you observe, the snake looks like a rubber snake. When you carefully see it, it is a rubber snake. What happens to you now? You get thoughts 'thank god, it is a rubber snake' or 'oh! I was so scared looking at a rubber snake. How stupid'. You feel a relief as soon as you realise it is not a real snake. You may laugh at yourself when the thought of getting scared looking at a rubber snake crosses your mind. Now, you may just continue to walk on the same path.

Imagine, you saw the snake, and got scared. Then you realise it is a rubber snake. You see a small group of kids hiding little away from the snake, looking at you and laughing. You realise that kids are trying to prank on you. What happens to you? If you think after all they are kids and having some fun. You may act as if you are scared and laugh with them. If you think kids are trying to make fun of you, you may get angry and scold them.

In the above scenario, each of us may react differently. But the reason why we react in a certain way is interesting.

When we see a snake, a thought is generated in our minds based on our knowledge about the snake and our previous experience. We know that snakes are poisonous, if snake bites, we may die. This thought leads to the emotion of fear. Because of the fear, we try to avoid the snake and take a different route.

But, once we realise it is not a real snake, a thought is generated that it is not a real snake and hence we are safe. This may lead us to feel a sense of relief. This feeling makes us continue in the same route.

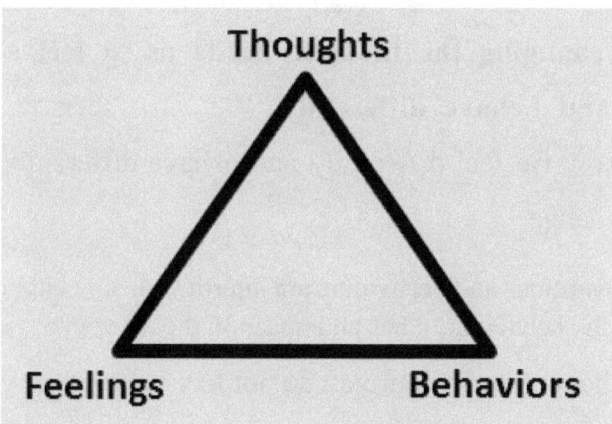

When we realize that kids are making a prank, if we think that after all they are kids, they are just having fun. We enjoy their prank, participate in that and laugh. If we think that playing a prank is wrong or how dare kids do a prank on me, we may get angry and that anger can lead us to shout or scold the kids.

From all the three scenarios mentioned above, what is the common thing? When there is any trigger(situation), a thought is generated in the human mind. That thought creates an emotion and eventually it drives the human to behave in a certain way.

What if we don't like our behaviour? What if our behaviours are not helping us reach our goals?

What to do if our emotions are troubling us? What if they are not pleasant? Araon Beck, the founder of Cognitive Behavioural Therapy (CBT) has found a model called **The Cognitive Triangle**, in which he describes how our thoughts influence the way we feel and subsequently how we act. And it is a continuous process.

Aron Beck also has given tools through CBT to address the negative pattern of thinking and behaving in an unhelpful manner. **According to CBT, changing the thoughts leads us to feel a different emotion and behave differently.** We have seen in the snake example how we feel differently and behave differently when our thoughts change.

Thoughts, emotions and behaviours are interlinked. You either change the thought or the behaviour, it has an impact on the other two.

Think of that one behaviour you do not like in you. Are you finding it difficult to change that behaviour? Take a deep breath and recollect the thoughts you get when you show that behaviour. What are those thoughts?

Write down your thoughts. Connect the dots. You have the key to change your behaviour or your emotion. You can make a choice!

8
Action Speaks Louder Than Words

Achal is 5 years old, living with parents and grandparents. He is an inquisitive kid who is curious about new things and does not hesitate to ask questions. He talks well, has friends at school and neighbourhood. He talks to his mother non-stop when he is around her, and has his own set of activities with grandparents. However, he becomes silent when his dad is around. His dad likes to spend more time with Achal. But Achal gives monosyllabic responses to his dad, he does not ask questions to him and usually avoids interactions with his dad. Worried about this, Achal's parents go to a counsellor along with him as per their paediatrician's advice.

Vandana and Varun have been married for a year now. There are constant fights between them in a span of a year. It was an arranged marriage. Vandana gets triggered and gets angry after most of the conversations with Varun and his mother. She talks well and has a good bonding with her father-in-law. Fights between Varun and Vandana reached a stage where they decided to consult a family therapist.

Anantha was upset after the meeting with his boss. He was a director in a MNC with 25 years of experience. He joined the MNC 2 years back after 23 years of experience in small companies. In the last 2 years, there were a lot of complaints against Anantha by his reporters. This time, it had reached the leadership team and his boss had recommended Anatha to get coached by an internal coach for communication.

On visit to the counsellor and coach in the above cases, it was found that one of the components which led to the issue was communication skills.

During the counselling, Achal's parents came to know that Achal was hesitant to talk freely with his dad as he used to panic by the tone of his dad. His dad's voice was loud and whenever he was not accepting the child's behaviour, he used to raise his voice. Achal felt threatened with the tone of his dad. Gradually, he started avoiding interactions with dad as a coping mechanism.

Varun and his mother had typical ways of facial expression and hand gestures while they talked. This annoyed Vandana. Also, their pace of talk used to become fast and loud when they were stressed or under pressure. During the counselling session, it was discovered that Vandana felt rejected with those facial expressions and hand gestures. The loud voice led her to an anxious state.

Anantha, who was upset with the complaints from his reporters, checked with his boss on what exactly was his reporters complaining about his communication skills. His reporters had complained about the way he gave feedback, some of the specific words he used, his tone of voice and his body language. When any work was not delivered, Anantha used to get angry and felt to show a sense of power. This led him to yell at his reportees. When he accused his reporters, he used to make hand gestures which intimidated them. In the meetings, the way he used to sit used to show authority and power which used to irritate his reporters.

Communication is not language. Webster's dictionary defines communication as 'a process by which information is exchanged between individuals through a common system of symbols, signs, or behaviour'. As the definition says, communication is not just the words one uses. In fact, according to Albert Mehrabian, communication has three elements. He calls it a 7-38-55% rule for personal communication.

According to this rule communication happens in three ways as one talks.

1. **Choice Of Words:** The words one uses to communicate makes up to 7% of the communication

2. **Voice:** the pitch, tone, volume and pace of the voice makes up to 38% of the communication

3. **Body Language:** the visible actions seen by others using all the body parts makes up to 55% of the communication

During the counselling sessions for Achal & Vandana and their families, one of the important factors identified for Achal's parents and Varun and Varun's mother to work on their communication. They were asked to be mindful about their voice and body language along with words used while talking. They were also taught assertive communication skills. They were taught to recognise the emotions and express them instead of showing in their voice or body language. They were suggested to get further counselling done to process the emotions behind the tone and body language used.

Anatha went through a series of coaching sessions from a communication coach to learn the effective and empathetic communication techniques and explore his belief on power and authority.

Communication is not just a tool to exchange information. It helps in building trust and relationships. It helps in solving problems, making decisions, increase the knowledge and making better choices in life.

The unsaid things can have a deeper and longer impact than the said things. Let us be mindful of what we say, our voice and our body language.

9
What Does Losing A Job Means To You?

There was a change in Ravichandra's daily routine from the last six months. He was hardly sleeping. He had started eating more than what he used to do. He was disinterested in the activities he liked before. Ravichandra lost his job and position as a director in a MNC due to recession. This came as a jolt for his identity and hit his self-esteem badly. As there was an ongoing recession, he could not get a job as his remuneration was above the market standards.

Ravichandra was well settled by the age of 45, with loan free assets. He was in a position to manage the same lifestyle without earning for a few years. But he associated his work and position with his identity. Loss of job meant loss of his identity. This led him to deep sadness. The prolonged sadness led to depression and grief due to job loss.

Vishwanath's anger had increased over the last three months. He retired as a Superintendent Engineer from the public sector company five months ago. As he started to spend more time with his family and friends, he started realising that neither his family nor his friends took his orders or followed his advice. Vishwanath, being in a high position for a few years, power and authority were something he was very much used to. One of his friends even made a statement that, 'hey man, now you are a retired person and one among us. You cannot command us to do something like you did in your office'. That hurt Vishwanath's ego with a stark realisation. Vishwanath went through a series of emotions like anger, frustration, irritation and helplessness.

Vishwanath's daughter who lived close by sensed how the retirement has affected her father. She suggested he take up a community initiative and lead it. Her idea was to engage him towards a purpose and utilise his skills and time in a constructive manner. Vishwanath was initially not interested with this idea but slowly started getting involved in community activities.

Suhas had a lot of free time for the last month. He lost IT job due to performance issues. Initially, Suhas was very sad, hurt and felt helpless. In the last five years in IT, he always struggled to deliver his work on time with quality. He was hardworking, committed and dedicated to work. But somehow, he could not cope with the kind of work and pressure the IT job was demanding. Suhas had foreseen losing the job in future. So Suhas had saved enough money to sustain the monthly expenses for six months. His wife was earning and his father used to get a pension. So Suhas didn't feel the financial burden as much and his family understood his situation and supported him financially and emotionally.

Instead of looking for another IT job, Suhas spent time in retrospection, the last five years of his career. With introspection, he felt he may not fit for an IT job. But he was not sure what job would suit him and he didn't know what else he could take up as a job. That is when he met his old friend who was a career coach. He took career coaching for three months to find what he is good at and what career may suit him. After six months, Suhas has applied for a branded apparel franchise and is working towards having his own outlet.

In the above cases, one common thing you can see is all three of them have lost their job. The way each of them have dealt with the job loss is different and hence the results. It is normal to grieve after a job loss, similar to the grief due to the death of a loved one. Some people may accept the job loss and move on. For few, it may be very difficult to accept and it may impact their physical and mental health and even relationships. It also can affect one's confidence and self-esteem.

How Do We Know One Is Grieving from Job Loss?

Job loss can lead to different emotions. These emotions may lead to different behaviours. Below are the few patterns of grief:

- Feeling sad or depressed
- Feeling angry and irritated
- Feeling hurt and worthless
- Feeling denial of the job loss
- Change in sleeping and eating patterns

- Difficulty concentrating in daily routine
- Lack of interest in activities which was enjoyable earlier
- Lack of energy to do any task
- Financial stress

Ravichandra, Vishwanath and Suhas, all three lost their jobs for different reasons but one thing common among them was grief due to job loss. The way each of them coped with it is also different.

Based on their stories we can categorise job loss into three categories, but the same coping mechanisms may apply to them.

Job loss, be it due to retirement, recession or performance issues can lead to a range of emotions like anger, hurt, sadness, guilt, anxiety, fear, disappointment, frustration, self-esteem issues and so on. Emotions depend on how a person equates to the job and need of the job. It is important to acknowledge how one feels after losing a job. Accept the different emotions to move forward. Anticipating the probable challenges post job loss and being prepared for it helps to cope up better without getting stuck in a grief cycle.

Financial preparation, a constructive plan for a new routine and finding a purpose can help to deal with the job loss positively.

Tips To Deal with A Job Loss:

1. Give yourself permission to grieve the job loss but do not dwell on it: Recognize the emotions, talk with family or a trusted friend about how you feel with respect to the loss.

Releasing the pent-up emotions is like a pressure cooker. You release the pressure now and then to avoid an outburst.

2. Accept the reality: Only once the situation is accepted, one will be able to go to the next stage. Accepting helps to think and plan for the future and move forward.

3. Being financially prepared for the situation puts less stress after retirement or an unexpected job loss. In case of retirement, clearing the loans and liabilities before retirement, having an idea about the expenses post-retirement and financial preparedness for it reduces the mental burden of money needs. In the case of private jobs, fields where layoffs are common, financially being prepared to lead a life with the same lifestyle for 6 months without a job helps to deal with grief and also focus on finding another job peacefully.

4. Importance of routine: Plan the new routine - how to utilise the time constructively. Knowing how to spend the sudden extra time in hand keeps one busy and avoids unnecessary brooding over the job loss.

5. Explore opportunities: Look for opportunities to either earn or to do something fulfilling based on one's needs. It could be finding another job, volunteering for community work, exploring oneself with hobbies and so on.

6. Focus on your health: It is very important to take care of physical health and mental health. It may take some time to find a new job, decide on how to spend your retired life. Being healthy allows one to think clearly.

7. Reach out for support: If none of these strategies work and grief is prolonged beyond three months, reach out to a professional counsellor.

Change is the only constant thing in life. Adapt and adjust and move forward!

10
Management Of Grief

Suguna heard the news of the death of her cousin's husband. He was just forty-five and Suguna was shocked to hear the news. It was unbelievable that her cousin's husband is no more. Her cousin, Swetha, just turned forty-one last week. Suguna lived in the States and it was not possible to fly immediately to meet her cousin. She picked up the phone and dialled her cousin's number. But she cut the call immediately. She didn't know how to start the conversation with her grieving cousin or what to say.

Jennifer got a message from Rohit that he would be back in the office the next day. Rohit was in Jennifer's team. He had lost his wife in an accident three weeks back. Jennifer's first thought after seeing the message was how to start a conversation with Rohit. Jennifer was thinking if he asked 'how did all that happen', 'how is he doing now' may remind Rohit of his wife and increase grief. Jennifer was really concerned about Rohit. He didn't know what is the appropriate way to show his concern and condolences to Rohit.

Mahesh heard from Rekha (Rakesh's sister), that their mother passed away. Rakesh was very attached to his mother. Mahesh knew how shocking and painful it was for Rakesh to lose his mother. Mahesh wanted to be there for Rakesh. Mahesh immediately called Rakesh to talk to him. Even after multiple rings and messages he didn't respond. He started getting ready to go to Rakesh's place. He received a message from Rekha requesting him not to call or meet Rakesh for a few days. It was a request from Rakesh. Mahesh could not just believe this.

It is very common for all of us to face a situation similar to what Suguna, Jennifer and Mahesh faced. What do we do when we hear the death news from people who have lost their loved ones? We express our condolences. When we do not know what to say, we say the standard statements like 'May the soul rest in peace', 'May God give you strength and courage to cope with the loss' and so on. Expressing condolences over the email or chat is relatively easier. What if you need to talk to someone very close to you, like Suguna and Mahesh or someone with whom you spend most of the time in a day, like Jennifer? Are we equipped for that sensitive talk? Do we know what will help the other person to feel understood? Or what kind of help they may need to process their grief? Many of us struggle with this. We may avoid talking to them. Some of us may use the standard statements used, 'Be strong', 'He is in a better place now', 'She was so good, God also wanted her' and so on.

Grief is triggered as an event of loss. Loss can be the death of a loved one (including a pet), divorce, relationship loss, miscarriage or even job loss. In this article, we are focusing more on grief generated due to the loss of a loved one. Grief is a natural response to loss. Grief is defined as emotional suffering when something or someone we love is taken away. It is a cognitive, emotional, behavioural and functional response to any loss. A person who is grieving goes through a range of emotions based on their equation with the person they lost. It could be intense sorrow, anger, fear, anxiety, hurt, guilt, shame and so on. Each individual may grieve differently. Based on the personality type, one may want space and want to process their emotions on their own or some people prefer to talk about what happened and how they are feeling. Some people may even reach out for professional help. In grief therapy, therapists help the client to navigate through different stages of grief before coming to the acceptance stage. Kubler Ross, a psychiatrist has come up with five stages of grief - Denial, Anger, Bargaining, Depression & Acceptance.

When we have a grieving relative, friend or a colleague, we would be concerned about that person and want to talk to them, help them. As said earlier, there is no standard protocol for grieving. It is very individualistic. As a well-wisher, we need to leave that choice to the grieving person and respect their choice. We can assure we are there for them, if they need help. We can tell them we are available to listen to them if they feel like talking. Giving that choice helps them to reach out for help when they need it.

A grieving person may need help to run some errands in the initial days of the death. When we ask them if they need help, they may not be in a position to tell what kind of help they want. Even if they ask, we may not be able to help them in that way. So, it is better to offer specific help to them. Ask them if you can cook for them that day. You can offer to buy the veggies or baby sit. If you want to help them financially, especially when a person has died after illness and hospitalisation, you can ask them if you can pay any hospital charges or cost of rituals.

A grieving person wants to be understood. In the grieving state, a person may not be able to think rationally, hence advice may not work. Giving personal examples of coming out of grief may not help as the person does not feel understood.

It is common for most of us to feel uncomfortable or unequipped to start a conversation with a grieving person in a way the person feels understood. Here are some examples from a study of what is an appropriate way of talking and what may be inappropriate in a conversation with a grieving person.

Grieving Person May Feel Not Understood By The Below Statements

1. At least she lived a long life, many people die young.
2. He is in a better place.
3. She brought this on herself.
4. There is a reason for everything.
5. It has been a year now that he passed - away. It is time to move on.

6. You can have another child.

7. She was such a good person God wanted her to be with him

8. I know how you feel.

9. She did what she came here to do and it was her time to go.

10. Be strong.

11. It is all God's wish.

12. Think about your kids' future - You need to be courageous at least for that.

13. Time will heal.

Appropriate Statements To Make The Grieving Person Feel Understood:

1. I am so sorry for your loss.

2. I wish I had the right words; just know I care.

3. I don't know how you feel, but I am here to help in any way I can.

4. You and your loved one will be in my thoughts and prayers.

5. My favourite memory of your loved one is…

6. I am always just a phone call away.

7. We all need help at times like this, I am here for you.

8. I am usually up early or late, if you need anything.

9. You can call or message me when you feel like talking.

10. I am going to the grocery store, do you want me to pick up anything for you?

11. Wanted to check if it is okay if I get dinner for you guys.

12. Do you want to talk about it? I am here to listen (And no advice please).

13. Give a hug instead of saying something.

14. Saying nothing, just be with the person.

Putting ourselves in the shoes of the griever gives us an idea of what words can help to feel understood. If you are going to talk to a person who is grieving, be mindful of your words, be sensitive and prepare yourself before you talk to them. Listening empathetically and non-judgmentally are powerful tools. If you see a person grieving beyond 3-6 months, guide them to seek professional help.

Loss and grief are inevitable. We cannot avoid them. But we can make the grieving person feel understood by empathetic and non-judgemental listening. Be supportive and give help.

Words are powerful. They can make a huge impact. They can bring changes. Choose your words mindfully.

11
Suspicious Personality & Relationships

Mohan and Bhavana were waiting at the counselling centre for their turn. Bhavana was tired. Occasionally, tears kept rolling out of her eyes. Mohan was stressed and overwhelmed. As he was thinking, the receptionist walked up to them, 'You can go inside' showing the door which had a board 'Vishwanath - Marriage counsellor'.

After a brief introduction, counsellor asked them 'What brings you here?'.

Mohan cleared his throat, 'Sir, we have been married for six years. It was an arranged marriage. Both of us are into IT, she is a sales manager and I am a techie. We lived in the UK for two years. I lost my father four years back and my mother became alone after that. Hence, we moved to India. After moving here, we have started fighting. Fights have become more frequent and serious. I don't know if we still love each other. So, we are here to sort out things said in a shaky voice.

The counsellor nodded and turned to Bhavana. She was crying. The counsellor offered her some tissues and waited.

'I love him so much sir. I don't have any issues with him. But I cannot take the allegations from my mother-in-law any more. I am fed up'

'So, you don't have any issue with your husband', the counsellor clarified.

'Yes sir. He is a nice person. We were so happy when we were in the UK. But things started to change once we moved to India', she looked at Mohan.

Mohan agreed with Bhavana in this matter. But he also thinks that there will be conflicts between mother-in-law and daughter-in-law. But Bhavana is blowing petty things out of proportion. According to Bhavana, there are serious allegations made by her mother-in-law on her character, which cannot be considered as petty things.

Mohan shared a recent incident, 'This morning my mother asked her whether she had misplaced the cooker. For that she picked up a fight saying 'your mother is suspicious'.

Bhavana was fuming, 'Why are you telling this small incident? Share other incidents where she has accused me?',

'Can you please allow me to complete?' Mohan snapped back.

As per Mohan's perspective, Bhavana gets annoyed for small things such as his mother asking whether they had dinner outside, where is the remote kept and so on. He complained that in any incident, she would link the past incidents and make it bigger. Bhavana said he was only giving a partial picture and not a complete one.

She explained briefly how she was irritated by her mother-in-law's way of talking in the initial days. She had ignored them considering her mother-in-law's age and loss. But after a year, things turned out to be intolerable. One day, when she had gone for an office party, her mother-in-law called her and accused her of having stolen her slippers. She was so annoyed that day. Her mother-in-law's accusations were baseless and irrational.

In another incident, her mother-in-law accused her of stealing her 300 rupees saree. Bhavana made a big issue out of it with Mohan. She was fuming with anger. Why on earth someone earning a big salary would steal a 300 rupees saree. When Mohan tried to talk to his mother, she created a drama and things went out of his control.

As Bhavana was explaining these incidents, Mohan was gazing at the floor.

Bhavana continued 'She has made all kinds of bad statements about me. I am into sales sir. As part of my job, I have to attend dinner parties with my clients. My mother-in-law has the habit of talking to herself. One day, when I came late, she was making a statement 'who knows where and who does she go with, what does she do. She just gives office as an excuse. She is a bitch'. She started crying profusely. 'tell me sir, can anyone take such allegations? He complains that I bring this every time we have a fight. How can I forget this?'.

'I see that these accusations have created a trauma in you. How do you react in such cases?' the counsellor probed gently.

'I get mad at both of them. I cry, I fight. I feel he is not supporting me enough. My mother-in-law is so irrational, I cannot argue with her'.

As the discussion with the counsellor continued, Bhavana realised that she gets angry on such occasions. Anger is due to the hurt of accusations. She feels sad because Mohan is unable to confront his mother. Bhavana also feels anxious to talk to her mother-in-law or do any household chores as her mother-in-law's behaviour is unpredictable. All these emotions lead to fights and breakdown. So, Bhavana has reduced her interaction with her mother-in-law in the recent past.

'Do you want to share anything Mohan?' counsellor checked with Mohan.

Mohan with a heavy heart explained how he felt guilty of his inability to make his mother understand that her behaviour is causing stress in the family. He felt angry and helpless. He was also anxious about having any conversation with his mother or wife.

Bhavana started feeling better as Mohan expressed what he was going through.

She asked the counsellor in a curious tone. 'I wonder what makes my mother-in-law behave that way sir?'

The counsellor acknowledged her question and enquired with Mohan whether he had seen any pattern in his mother's suspicious nature. Mohan recollected how his mother does not trust him in money matters, she fears that he may steal her money, keeps repeatedly going to the bank to check if her money is safe. He also recollected that she was very suspicious about her father and had accused him repeatedly of having an affair.

The counsellor asked if Mohan knew anyone on his mother's side having paranoid behaviour. Mohan remembered his maternal uncle who was paranoid. His wife had divorced him due to this nature.

Hearing this Bhavana asked, 'Do you think this is hereditary?'

'We will discuss more about this in the next session. We will also discuss how to proceed with counselling'.

Mohan and Bhavana thanked the counsellor and left. Both of them were feeling lighter. Bhavana held Mohan's hand, 'Can we have dinner outside today?'

'I will call Amma and inform her', he took out his mobile to call. Bhavana was thinking when was the last time they had a simple conversation like this without an argument. She was looking forward to the next session with the counsellor.

Next week, when Bhavana & Mohan came into the counselling, the counsellor observed that they were in a better mood.

Bhavana started the conversation with enthusiasm. 'After the last session, we were discussing my mother-in-law's suspicious nature. Mohan also shared what his father went through and how it has affected Mohan. Mohan has seen both of them getting into fights whenever my father-in-law confronted her. And it had not led to any constructive talks. So, Mohan does not confront her which used to irritate me a lot'.

'Yes, but I never realised that discussing these things with her would help us to understand each other better', Mohan said in a calm tone.

'We would like to know more about how we can understand each other better and strengthen our relationship', Bhavana looked at Mohan as he nodded in agreement.

The counsellor said with a smile, 'Thanks for sharing this'.

'We want to know what my mother's problem is and whether it can be treated. Also, we are open to get counselled if that helps.

'Wonderful Mohan, that makes my work easier'. counsellor then educated about the suspicious nature of Mohan's mother, how some people show a pattern of distrust and suspicion of others without adequate reason to be suspicious. They feel that others are constantly trying to deceive or harm them. These kinds of people do not think their behaviour is problematic. Hence getting them help through treatment or counselling is a challenge.

Mohan and Bhavana understood the mental health condition Mohan's mother has. They were concerned about it. Yet there was relief in knowing why she behaves in a suspicious way.

The counsellor also mentioned that Bhavana would need counselling as these incidents have been very traumatic and that needs to be processed through the sessions. Along with individual therapy for Bhavana, he recommended couple therapy which can help them in understanding each other better, sort conflicts amicably and learn to communicate better.

'Thank you so much sir. When can I have individual therapy?' Bhavana asked eagerly. While leaving the centre, she also mentioned that she is positive about dealing with similar incidents in the future in a better way.

Bhavana was on individual therapy for three months and was able to process the trauma. She learnt techniques on how to deal with her anger, anxiety and hurt feelings during the therapy sessions. Although her mother-in-law continues to show the same behaviour. Bhavana is able to deal with the situations with lesser impact on her.

Mohan and Bhavana have started a couple therapy, and started enjoying knowing each other better.

12

When There Is A Roadblock On The Memory Lane

Nisha was early to the office that day. She was eagerly waiting for Shachi to review the final version of the slide deck prepared for the client meeting. The meeting was in the second half of the day. Nisha wanted to make sure she had enough time to make any last-minute changes to the slides. It was 10.30am already and Shachi had not come to the office yet. She checked her WhatsApp messages to see if Shachi had responded to her. There was no response from Shachi. She had not picked up Nisha's calls as well. Nisha was a little upset with no communication from Shachi. She also felt a little uneasy as Shachi usually responds very quickly. She was thinking, if something had gone wrong at Shachi's side.

She decided to give herself a caffeine boost quickly to deal with stress and nervousness of the client meeting. Though, Nisha was not the primary person who is supposed to present the slide, she was told that parts of the presentations to be given by her, while Shachi takes the lead.

She went to the cafeteria to meet Ravi, her and Shachi's boss. She waved at Ravi as he saw her from the corner of the cafeteria. It seemed like Ravi was stressed too. She took the coffee and went towards his table. Ravi was drinking coffee and writing something on his laptop. As she pulled the chair to sit opposite to Ravi, he looked up and in a tense voice asked, 'did you hear the news from Shachi?'

Clueless Nisha, shook her head horizontally and asked in an anxious voice, 'What happened? Is everything alright? She is not responding to my calls and messages. I have been waiting for her for an hour'. Nisha bombarded Ravi with multiple questions at once, releasing all her pent-up stress from morning.

'Shachi's father has been missing since morning it seems. They are looking for him around', Ravi leaned towards Nisha and said in a low voice.

'Oh No..', Nisha literally shivered upon hearing this news. A light sweat was visible on her forehead. She seemed instantly disturbed.

'Are you okay Nisha? Do you want some water?' Ravi offered water to her, noticing the sudden changes in Nisha. She drank water and sat in silence for a minute. She regained her composure, 'Now I am okay Ravi. A year back my father went missing for a day and that memory suddenly flooded me. We were so afraid and anxious the whole day'. She changed her position and suddenly there was a positive shift to her energy and voice. 'If you are talking to her, can you ask her to call me? I think I can also share a few things which helped us to find my father then'. Ravi nodded his head, 'I will text her right away' and messaged Shachi.

'Nisha, coming back to the presentation, as Shachi has this situation, we need to find an alternate person to lead the discussion. I was wondering whether you could handle this? You have been involved in every meeting till now and also you are the one who have prepared the slide. I could not think of any other person better suited to handle this? What are your thoughts?'

In any other situation, Nisha would have felt mixed emotions with this sudden opportunity. But Nisha was thinking about Shachi's situation and with a determination she said, 'Yes Ravi, I will handle this. I may need your help and support. I may not be as good as Shachi in leading this, but I will give my best. Please review the final version of the slide and let me know if any changes are required'. Ravi nodded and said 'I will reply in the next thirty minutes.

As Nisha reached her desk, her mobile rang. It was Shachi. She received the call.

'Hi Nisha, sorry I could not call you back earlier or reply to your messages', there was tension in Shachi's voice. Nisha took a deep breath, 'That is okay Shachi. Ravi told me about your father going missing'. She paused. 'Yes Nisha, we are all so worried and tensed here. My husband and brother have gone out to search for him. My father went out to bring milk at 6am in the morning. Milk shop is five minutes' walk from the house. When he didn't return, even around 9am, my mom tried to call him. He has not taken mobile as well. Then she called me and my brother and we came here immediately'. She paused to take a breath. Nisha took that moment, 'We are also worried and concerned Shachi. Let us see how soon we can find your dad. Did you check with your mother about how your dad was when he left home in the morning?'

Nisha could hear a sigh from Shachi, 'My dad had forgotten to keep the milk coupon at night it seems. My mother wants coffee first thing in the morning. So, both of them have fought regarding not keeping the milk coupon. I don't know if my father got angry and left the house'. There was a pause and Shachi had broken down. 'Sorry Nisha, I could not control myself. I am putting a brave face in front of my mother and have held up my worries from morning', Shachi continued. 'We inquired in the regular milk shop from where we buy milk. He has not gone there. That is really worrying us. We are wondering if he left home in anger over the fight in the morning'.

'Okay, so after the fight, did he say he is going out to buy milk?', Nisha enquired.

'It seems he asked for the exact change for the milk with Amma. This is so confusing'. Shachi was thinking and talking simultaneously.

'Okay Shachi, tell me one thing. Did your dad have memory issues?' Nisha asked.

'Not really'. After a pause, 'You mean whether he forgot things?'.

'Exactly Shachi. Did he find it difficult to remember certain things?' Nisha probed Shachi.

'Well. Sometimes yes. But Amma used to tell that he was acting up. He remembered well what the dish was made on a certain day 15 years back. Which colour saree Amma wore for their 5th anniversary types. But he used to say he forgot his mobile, keys and specs. He used to misplace things and search for them. So Amma used to scold him for being absent minded. Not paying attention to what she says. He used to discuss some errands to be done with Amma and then later forget about it completely. But why are you asking this Nisha?' Shachi asked anxiously.

'I was wondering if he forgot the way back home. Hold on, Ravi is calling. I will put you on hold', Nisha switched the call to speak to Ravi. She connected back to Shachi after a couple of minutes.

'It seems client meetings are cancelled today as the client has some crisis at the office. Ravi called to update on that', Nisha updated Shachi.

'That is good. I was feeling guilty that I put things on you, suddenly', Shachi confessed.

'Let's come back to your dad. Shachi, I can so well relate to what you are going through, as I was in a similar situation a year ago. My dad went missing and it was really a tough time for us to find him back'. Nisha's voice lowered.

'So, you found him back? That's good. How long did it take?', Shachi was now curious and hopeful.

Nisha paused and shared, 'It took about a day for us to find him. That is because we didn't act thoroughly from the time, he went missing. We also thought he was angry at us as we had not agreed on certain things my father wanted at our new house. So, we lost quite some time on discussing and debating what could be the reason he went missing'.

'Oh, hearing this I am feeling hopeful as well as scared. What do I do Nisha now? Is there anything else we could do to find him soon?' Shachi now started thinking on actions.

'One thing which helped us is to circulate his pic in social media with contact numbers to call. Another thing is lodging a complaint in a police station. This would expedite getting any leads. This is what helped us to find my dad'. Nisha shared her experience.

'Shachi, my brother is calling. Thank you so much for your suggestions. I will discuss this at home and take action. I will call you back', Shachi hung up and Nisha got back to work reluctantly.

Nisha kept checking with Shachi on the progress until evening. She left the office in the evening, emotionally disturbed. She got a call from Shachi around 8.45pm while preparing for dinner.

'Nisha, we found my dad. Such a relief. Thank you so much for your help. Your guess was right Nisha. He seemed to be a little off. It seems he was not able to remember the route to the milk shop and had trailed off to Kanakapura road. Then he was not able to remember where our house was. Luckily someone who read the social media post recognized him near Konanakunte cross. He made a video call and my dad recognized us and started crying. We went and brought him from there', Shachi started sobbing.

'So relieved to hear this, Shachi. Take rest and take care of my uncle. It has been a long and tiring day for you guys. Call me tomorrow without fail'. Nisha hung the phone with relief.

Next two days Shachi didn't go to the office. But she and Nisha had a long talk. Nisha shared her experience about how her father was diagnosed with Alzheimer's dementia after that incident of him going missing. They consulted a neurologist and later a psychiatrist to confirm the diagnosis. Nisha shared what she knew about Alzheimer's dementia - a progressive disease that destroys memory and other important mental functions.

Dementia affects memory, thinking and reasoning, making judgements and decisions, planning and performing familiar tasks. It also brings changes in personality. She also remembered how her father went into depression and showed apathy. How he had developed suspicion and mistrust about others. She shared that recently he had started seeing people who are not in the room. Feels that someone is there to harm him and tries to go out of the house even in mid-nights.

Shachi could relate to a few symptoms which her father was showing. She and her brother took her father to a neurologist and it was confirmed that there was an onset of dementia for her father after a series of cognitive and mental status examination tests. Doctor also explained that it is a degenerative disease which does not have a cure as of now. But the treatment helps in slowing down the progression of the disease.

Shachi's dad has been prescribed medication and some lifestyle changes. The family is counselled to understand dementia, different stages and what they can expect from her dad, in the future. They were also taught some questionnaires to help her dad to keep oriented with space and time and active.

Unlike Nisha's father, Shachi's father does not need a full-time caretaker as the disease is still in early stages. Shachi's family is slowly getting used to the new ways of supporting her father.

Why Is It Important To Know About Dementia?

Though symptoms of dementia can be categorised clearly as something outside normal way of thinking and behaving, there is a tendency for people to brush it under the carpet as absenteeism, selective memory and age-related issues. Ignoring and delaying the treatment can put the family in significant stress.

As per WHO, worldwide, around 55 million people have dementia. As the proportion of older people in the population is increasing in nearly every country, this number is expected to rise to 78 million in 2030 and 139 million in 2050. In India also, elderly people are developing Dementia as in the West.

Three major types of Dementia:

1. ALZIEMER's Dementia:

Decline in the number of neurons and neurotransmitter Acetylcholine lead to this type. Cause is not known.

2. Vascular Dementia:

Poor blood supply, blood clots, bleeding inside the brain due to poorly treated diabetes and high BP.

3. Alcohol and Intoxicating drug induced Dementia:

Impact of dementia is multi-dimensional. Apart from the person who has dementia, the whole family gets affected. It also affects the person's family physically, emotionally, socially & economically. This can lead to a lot of stress for the family. As per a study in 2019, informal carers spend an average 5 hours a day providing care for people with dementia.

Primary caretakers of dementia also need counselling to deal with their stress and keep their mental health in check. There are also options to hire full time help, day care centres and rehab centres based on the one's needs and affordability.

In a nutshell, seeking professional help, helps both the person and family to deal with dementia challenges in a better way and improves the quality of life.

13
Care For The Caregiver

Radha's life has completely changed after her second child was born. She had felt the joy and satisfaction of becoming a mother again. The first six months went by sleepless nights taking care of the baby 24/7 and managing the elder child. The joy slowly faded and occasional worries crept in, as she noticed that her son was lagging behind other babies of his age in terms of motor movements. Her anxiety peaked when he turned one and half and not meeting the significant milestones of his development in terms of crawling, standing and walking. On consulting doctors and getting tests done, her son was diagnosed with Cerebral Palsy, a group of disorders which affects a person's ability to move and maintain balance and posture.

In the last five years, Radha had to quit her job to take care of her son. This had also led to change school for her daughter due to financial strain in the family. She is juggling between household tasks, taking care of her husband and daughter. Most of the days, her day ends with physical and emotional exhaustion. Frequently she is haunted with guilt that she is unable to take care of her parents, who solely depend on her in their old age.

Mahesh was devastated when he heard his mother was diagnosed with cancer. He was brought up by his mother all alone as his father succumbed to an accident when he was two. When Mahesh realised that her mother was not going to survive for long, he went through intense anxiety, depression and guilt. He wanted to give the best to her. With his high paying job, good insurance coverage, Mahesh managed to get the best of the treatments for his mother. He hired a full-time help. In those 3 years of his mother's cancer diagnosis to her demise, Mahesh withered physically, emotionally. His relationship with his wife and career declined. Mahesh could not focus on anything other than his mother. He was unable to complete his work on time in the office. He was oblivious to the needs of his wife. His emotional drain led to physical issues. He did not find time to do anything apart from attending to his mother and work.

Ahana was twenty-eight and the only daughter. She came from a middle-class family and aspired to work and support her parents. She was insistent that she gets married only after settling in a good job. After an initial struggle, she found a job which was of her interest and paid decently. As she was settling in her new job and looking forward for a better life for her and her parents, Ahana's father was diagnosed with Parkinson's, a progressive nervous system disorder which affects the movement. He started losing balance, falling and hurting himself. In a years' time, he reached a stage where he could not manage himself without help. Ahana's sense of responsibility towards her parents, anticipated guilt of leaving her parents if she gets married, held up Ahana from deciding on her marriage. Ahana's mother was old too and both mother and daughter could not help her father on their own. Ahana hired a part time help. Her earnings soared in paying for treatment and the help. Their lifestyle was back to square-one. She was battling to prioritise her own needs with her role as a daughter. With part time help, though the falls of his father had reduced, there were one or the other things every day, which needed her attention and action. She was not able to focus on work. In the last two years, while her peers moved into the next role and got a good hike, Ahana stayed in the career ladder where she was when she joined. She experiences anxiety, anger, guilt and depression quite often.

Ashok meets his friends after a long time. He felt so good connecting with his friends after three years. He used to miss all the monthly and annual meets of his school and college friends. Many of his friends, who knew nothing about Ashok's personal life labelled him as 'family man' who does not give time for friends. Some of his friends were surprised to see him at the get-together. Some pulled his legs saying, how come Ashok's wife let him attend a party! Ashok felt not understood by his friends. He thought this was the time to share what happened to him and his family in the last three years. He shared about how his father was diagnosed with dementia, how he slowly lost all his cognitive abilities like memory, judging and perception. How his father forgot who he was and his family members. Ashok, briefly shared he was busy attending and taking care of his father along with other work and family responsibilities. Many of his friends expressed sorry for what his father had to go through. Some of them apologised for pulling his leg all these years for not attending the parties. Ashok noticed that none of his friends asked how he felt in the last three years, taking care of his father. In the last three years, Ashok has felt immense frustration, helplessness, anger and anxiety. The emotional turmoil and stress have significantly affected his physical health too.

There are only four kinds of people in this world: those who have been caregivers, those who are currently caregivers, those who will be caregivers and those who will need caregivers. Caregiving is universal.

Rosalynn Carter, Former First Lady of the United States

Each one of us would have been a caregiver for a loved one, one or the other time in our adult life.

Who Is A Caregiver?

As per American dictionary, Caregiver is someone who provides for the needs of children or of people who are ill or cannot provide for their own needs. A caregiver is a person who attends to the needs of a person who has short- or long-term illness, injury or disability either physical or mental.

A caregiver can be a spouse, parent, children, family member or even a professional help. Caregiving impacts the caregiver in different ways based on the relationship with the patient. Longer the period of caregiving, higher the impact on the caregiver.

Issues With Caregiving

Caregiving issues can affect a professional paid caregiver as well as an unpaid person who gives care to a loved one, a friend or a family member. Variety of issues stem from caregiving.

The common caregiving issues revolve around:

Primary issues:
- Physical issues
- Mental health issues

Secondary issues:
- Relationship issues
- Financial strain
- Setback in work
- Reduced quality life
- Lack of self-care
- Isolation, loneliness & apathy

Caregiving often results in chronic psychological stress. Based on the relationship and equation with the patient, the emotional state of the caregiver varies. One may experience intense anxiety and depression thinking about the worst. When the caregiving is forced or previous experiences with the patient is unpleasant, there could be a lot of anger the caregiver goes through.

Physical strain and long-term caregiving may lead to irritation and frustration to the caregiver. Because of the energy and time required for caregiving, caregivers may not be able to indulge in self-care activities like physical exercise, relaxation activities and so on leading to stress.

As the caregiving is taxing when it is long-term, a caregiver may not be able to spend quality time with other relationships like spouse, children or parents which may hamper those relationships. This may lead to emotions like guilt, hurt and anger.

Caregiver, if working may get stuck in the career growth as focusing the work and dedicating to career aspirations may not be possible. This also can contribute to the financial strain with no salary revisions. This again can lead to emotions like anxiety, frustration, disappointment, depression and so on.

One of the studies from Carers worldwide shows that there are 273 million caregivers in India alone. 84% of them are women and girls. 92% of the caregivers worry about money and 79% suffer from anxiety and depression.

A study shows that in India unpaid caregivers spend 24.6 hours a week in a week in caregiving activities. 3.5 hours a day goes into caregiving activities alone. The physical and emotional stress of caregiving consumes energy and time beyond 3.5 hours a day.

Care For Caregivers

It is equally important for the caregiver to take care of oneself along with caring for the patient, especially when the caregiver is a family member.

As we now know, caregivers go through a series of emotional issues. Processing these emotions in a safe place with an empathetic and non-judgemental listening can help the caregiver to ventilate the pent-up emotions. Caregivers can talk and share what they are going through, how they are feeling, their challenges with anyone they trust. The listener can listen and offer any help if they could and refrain from advice. Because the caregivers may not have options and look forward to someone who could listen and understand them. They can also talk to counsellors or psychologists to learn techniques to process their emotions on their own.

If the family of the patient is financially well, they can think of hiring full time or part time help, reducing the burden of the family member of their caregiving activities. There are a lot of agencies who provide professional help who are trained to give care for specific illnesses/disabilities. There are also long-term care centres for the sick. There are short term respite homes which give a temporary break and relief from caregiving for the caregiver and the family. One can explore the options based on their needs and affordability.

What Can You Do If You See A Caregiver?

Do you want to know how you can help a caregiver, if you come across one?

Just listen to them. Acknowledge them what they are going through. Ask them how they are dealing with the stress? Offer them small, specific help if you could. Refer them to a counsellor for professional help. Openly appreciate their work and dedication.

14
Speaking The Right Love Language

Menaka feels that her husband does not love her any more after ten years of their married life. In the first few years of their marriage, Ravi, Menaka's husband used to come home early, take Menaka out for dinner or to a movie. They used to travel and trek over the weekend and holidays. As the years passed by, their family grew with a daughter and son. Their responsibilities increased. Ravi also was growing in his career, with higher roles and responsibilities requiring more of his attention and time at work. From growing demands from his work to helping Menaka in her household tasks and taking care of kids, Ravi hardly got time for himself. Their routine changed from late evening dinners and movies to picking and dropping kids from school to tuitions. Attending kids' homework and health. There used to be one or the other thing every evening for Ravi, an unplanned meeting, breakdown of Menaka's car or one of the kids falling sick to attend.

The neighbours envied Menaka for the support and help she got from Ravi. But Menaka lately felt that Ravi is not giving her enough attention. He is not the same Ravi who loved her so much earlier.

Ravi's additional efforts to help Menaka in her household chores and taking care of kids did not make Menaka feel loved. For Menaka, Ravi spending time with her everyday was very important. She wanted Ravi to express his love by spending quality time with her.

For Ravi, expressing love was in the form of helping. In spite of his workload at office, Ravi made sure that he gets enough time to help Menaka in the kitchen, getting the kids ready for school and ensuring there is enough fuel in Menaka's car and so on. He felt that his love through helping her was never appreciated by Menaka.

Saanu was eight and threw tantrums like a four-year kid. From feeding to making her go to school, Saanu's mother Rekha had to try hard every day. Rekha felt anger and frustration about Saanu's behaviour. Rekha made efforts to take Saanu to the park every day. She took her to new places during weekends to give her daughter new experiences. She also bought a lot of gifts from toys to books for Saanu as a gesture of love. But Saanu seems not to understand how much Rekha loved her.

Saanu felt very good when she had a chance to sit on her mother's lap. She liked when she was hugged and kissed by people she loved. Rekha was born in a family where physical touch was not encouraged. Rekha didn't like when eight-year-old Saanu came and hugged or kissed her. She used to gently push Saanu aside when Saanu showed love to her mother through hugs and kisses. Saanu felt rejected by her mother whenever she was not reciprocated with hugs and kisses.

Vinay is a quick learner and very committed to work. He used to get motivated when he was praised for his work. But his boss was a perfectionist. Any small mistakes, his boss used to criticise him which demotivated Vinay. Though his boss ensured Vinay got a good hike and promotions for his hard work, Vinay felt very frustrated for not being appreciated for his work. In a span of two years, Vinay decided to quit his company to join a new one.

Love is a complex emotion consisting of intimacy, care, commitment, respect, trust, affection and attraction. Each of us expresses love in different forms. Do we feel loved by any gesture of love by others? Maybe not so.

Gary Chapman, an author, speaker and counsellor, with his wide range of experience with clients, says that different people with different personalities give and receive love in different ways. By learning to recognize these preferences in oneself and in their loved ones, one can learn to identify the root of the conflicts, connect more profoundly, and truly begin to grow closer. He has classified the expression of love into majorly five categories called love languages.

Words Of Affirmation

People with this type of love language value verbal acknowledgments of affection and appreciation. It could be a gratitude note like 'Thank you', words of encouragement - 'Well-done' or expression of affection - 'I love you'.

Quality Time

People whose love language is quality time feel most loved when their loved ones actively spend time with them. Spending quality time does not always mean a vacation or going for dinner. Giving undivided attention, going for a walk together or even by cleaning dishes together, quality time can be spent without distractions.

Acts Of Services

People with love language as acts of service, value when their loved ones go out of their way to make your life easier. It can be getting your loved one a glass of water when she is watching her favourite TV show, making a coffee in the morning or reminding him to take the umbrella.

Gifts

Gifts is a straightforward love language. People feel loved when others give a visual symbol of love. It's not about the monetary value but the thought behind the item. Gifts can be as simple as baking a cake for your loved one, getting an ice cream on a hot day or making a greeting card.

Physical Touch

People with physical touch as love language feel loved and cared for with a hug or a kiss, pat on the back, holding hands or any physical touch gesture. Physical touch need not be only romantic between partners.

How To Find Your Love Language?

There are online quizzes to find one's love language and you could take the test to find out your primary love language. Another way is to carefully observe yourself and find out which of the five love languages you are using on others. That will be your primary love language.

Once your find the primary love language, you need to request your loved ones to express their love in these forms. Before that, it is recommended to find out your loved one's love language and make efforts to express your love the way they want it.

Love at first sight happens. Sustaining love requires everyday commitment and effort.

'In fact, true love cannot begin until the in-love experience has run its course.' – Gary Chapman

15

Can Anxiety Influence Your Behaviour?

Saahi refused to go to school again. Meena was so angry that day, she hit her daughter with a scale for resisting to go to school. Saahi didn't budge. Instead, she started crying loudly. Meena gave in again and let Saahi stay at home.

Meena was worried. This was the fifth or sixth time Saahi was missing the school this year. Saahi is in fifth standard now. After two years of online classes due to the pandemic, now she has started going to school. It has been two months since the school has reopened. Saahi was very excited about going to school for the first two weeks. Then she started missing school once a week. Meena tried asking Saahi the reason for not wanting to go to school. Initially, she cited the reason for stomach pain. Meena believed initially but noticed that Saahi's symptoms vanished once she stayed back home. She spent the rest of the day playing video games, watching TV or painting. Meena double checked if Saahi was missing homework and not wanting to go to school. Saahi was a good student. Meena confirmed that Saahi had done all the home work.

Meena was very puzzled at her daughter's behaviour. This was new to her. Saahi never had missed school in the past giving fake reasons. Meena didn't know what to do. She was a single mother and didn't know whom to discuss this with. She was not comfortable discussing this with Saahi's teachers.

Meena remembered her schoolmate Reshma, who was a counsellor. She made a note to call her in the night and left a message to Reshma.

Next day, Saahi had a holiday as it was a Saturday. Meena prepared Poori Saagu, Saahi's favourite breakfast. As Saahi was enjoying her breakfast, Meena served some more saagu to Saahi and said,

'Saahi, this evening I am meeting one of my school friends at her clinic'.

Saahi looked up from her plate, 'Is she a doctor?' asked curiously.

Impressed by her daughter's keen listening, Meena responded with a smile, 'No, she is a psychologist'.

'Psychologist? What does she do?'

'Psychology is the study of minds. She helps people to deal with their mind related issues. You know Veena, counsellor mam in your school. She is also a psychologist'.

'Wow. but what kind of problems can a mind have?'

'That's a great question Saahi. Like our body, the mind can also get sick. Mind's sickness mostly revolves around the thinking, emotions and behaviours of the people'.

'That sounds interesting. I thought people go to counsellors when they score less. If anyone in my class scores very less marks, they are asked to meet Veena mam'.

'Really?'

'Yeah, also when kids are either bullied or bully others, they are also asked to meet her'.

'Hmm, have you ever got a chance to talk to her?' Meena probed.

'No, I have not scored less so far. Neither I bully anyone nor get bullied' Saahi replied with a smile.

Meena hugged her 'Do you want to join me to meet my friend Reshma today?'

Saahi thought for a moment, 'Probably, if Pinky is not available in the evening to play'.

Meena, 'Absolutely. You can also think about talking to Reshma aunty about your frequent stomach pain, if you come with me'.

Saahi raised her eyebrows, 'Stomach pain with a psychologist?'

Meena nodded and smiled. Saahi took her plate to the sink with a confused look on her face.

Meena and Saahi came to the Mind Grow Counselling centre at 5.15pm. As they were waiting in the reception, Saahi looked around to find a comic book titled, 'I wonder what makes people anxious?'. She started reading it curiously. By 5.30 pm, Meena was called inside. Meena asked Saahi whether she wants to come inside now or finish reading the book and join her. Saahi asked for five minutes so that she could complete reading the book.

Saahi knocked on the door of the counselling room. Reshma, opened the door and warmly welcomed Saahi, 'Hi Saahi, please come in. So good to see you'.

'Hi Aunty, thank you' Saahi replied quickly scanning the room.

'Did it bore you while you waited for Saahi?' Reshma initiated a conversation.

'No aunty, I was reading a comic'.

'That's nice. What were you reading?'

Before Saahi could answer, Meena interrupted. 'Sorry to interrupt. I am getting a call from the office. Must be something urgent. Saahi, is it okay if I step out for 10 minutes? I will join back once this call is over'.

Saahi nodded her head hesitantly.

'Take your time Meena', Reshma told Meena and turned to Saahi. 'We were talking about the comic. What did you learn from that book?'

Saahi changed her position 'when people get anxious, they may fight or avoid the stuff causing anxiety'.

Reshma lowered her tone, 'Have you experienced anxiety or fear recently Saahi?' Reshma chose her words carefully.

Shaahi's face changed and she seemed to be stressed. Reshma sensed it and assured she need not talk about it now, if she is not comfortable. Reshma talked about other stuff like school and play to make Saahi comfortable.

After two sessions with Reshma, Saahi opened up. Saahi had Karate classes every Friday. On Friday mornings, Saahi felt tired, her stomach used to hurt, her heart used to beat faster and she felt very uncomfortable. Once Saahi skipped school, all these symptoms vanished automatically.

Saahi was having anxiety over attending the Karate classes. Further conversations between Saahi & counsellor, it was discovered that Saahi had anxiety issues. Anxiety was stemming from various reasons. One of them was Saahi's earlier experience of witnessing her mother getting beaten by her father.

Reshma explained to Saahi and Meena about anxiety, how the autonomic nervous system goes to fight or flight mode when a person is anxious. She also explained how thinking can contribute to anxiety.

Meena took Karate class exemption for Saahi temporarily as per Reshma's recommendation and continued therapy for anxiety. After six months, Saahi was in a much better state to deal with her anxiety and started to attend the Karate classes.

16

How Can The Errors In Thinking Impact Us?

Have you noticed that even without doing any physical work, sitting at one place and thinking negatively can drain our energy? Or just by listening to people who have a negative outlook towards life.

Negative thinking can exhaust us like hard physical work. Isn't it? We all are negatively biassed in one or the other situation, in one or the other time. What is the reason?

Cognitive distortion/errors can be one of the reasons for our negative outlook towards life & negative thinking. A cognitive distortion is a mental process of acquiring knowledge and understanding the world often inaccurately and with a negative bias. Cognitive distortion gets developed over the years due to certain experiences in life.

Why Should We Really Worry About This?
Cognitive distortion can take a serious toll on mental health, can increase stress, anxiety & depression. It can impact the way one perceives the world and interacts with people. It can negatively influence the decisions one makes and the relationships!

If you have heard people saying 'Nobody loves me', 'I am not good at anything', 'I have no choice' and so on frequently, it may be coming from cognitive distortion of the mind.

Types Of Cognitive Distortion:

1. **All Or Nothing Thinking:** One looks at things in absolute black and white categories.

2. **Overgeneralization**: One views a negative event as a never-ending pattern of defeat.

3. **Mental Filter:** One dwells on the negative and ignores the positives.

4. **Discounting The Positives:** One insists that their accomplishments or positive qualities 'don't count'.

5. **Jumping To Conclusions:**

    a. Mind reading: One assumes that people are reacting negatively to them when there's no definite evidence for it.

    b. Fortune telling: One arbitrarily predicts things will turn out badly.

6. **Magnification Or Minimization:** One blows out things way out of proportion or they shrink their importance inappropriately.

7. **Emotional Reasoning**: One reason from how they feel: 'I feel like an idiot, so I really must be the one'.

8. **Should Statements**: One criticises self or other people with 'should' or 'shouldn't'. 'Musts', 'Have to's' and 'Ought's' give a similar effect.

9. **Labelling**: One identifies with one's shortcomings. Instead of saying 'I made a mistake', they label themselves as 'Idiots' or 'Stupid'.

10. **Personalization And Blame**: One blames self for something they were not responsible for or blame other people and overlook their attitudes and behaviours that contributed to the problem.

1. All Or Nothing Thinking:

A person with this type always thinks in extremes (black & white) and is unable to find alternate solutions to their problem. People with anxiety and depression may have such faulty thinking patterns.

For example, a person has successfully completed four years of graduation and attended a few interviews to get a job. On failing to clear a few job interviews, he may say 'My education is wasted because I am unable to get a job'.

2. Overgeneralization:

Overgeneralization causes errors in thinking leading to unnecessary emotional pain.

Error in thinking happens due to broad assumptions from limited experience, predicting the outcome of something based on just one instance. Prejudice is a form of overgeneralization.

Overgeneralization can demoralise and devastate the person and cause feelings of hopelessness.

Say, an employee's idea gets rejected in a discussion. With one incident, the employee thinks that her idea always gets rejected and stops sharing the ideas. Eventually, she may not give any ideas with this error in thinking.

A person messes up one presentation in the office and thinks 'he is not good at speaking and he always fails at giving good talks'. This kind of thinking will pull him away to attempt giving a presentation in the future.

Overgeneralization pulls the person away from achieving their goals. This also leads to others disliking this person for a lot of negativities.

3. Mental Filtering:

In an appraisal meeting, a person gets positive and negative feedback. The person feels very bad about the negative feedback and forgets or discounts the positive feedback. He sees his glass as half empty. Due to this, he feels either sad or anxious which further leads to other types of cognitive distortions.

Mental filtering is a type of cognitive distortion that creates faulty thought patterns similar to overgeneralization. People with this type of thinking have a tendency to filter out all the positives and focus only on the negatives. This leads to feelings of anxiety and sadness.

People with panic disorders are said to use mental filtering very frequently and discount all the pleasant and fulfilling factors of life and give more attention to inadequacies and dissatisfaction. They tend to feel lonely and show avoidance behaviours which is a learned behaviour to cope with panic disorder.

What Can We Do About Cognitive Distortion?

Journaling the thoughts helps to identify the distortions in thinking. It will help to easily identify the pattern and address it.

Challenging the thoughts through questions helps to reduce or be aware about one's cognitive distortion.

Examples of challenging the thoughts through questions:

'Nobody loves me':

- Really? Nobody?
- What makes you think so?

'I am not good in presenting to a larger audience':

- How many times you have presented to a larger audience?
- How many times it has gone wrong?

Cognitive Behavioural Therapy (CBT) helps to deal with cognitive distortions.

4. Discounting The Positives:

It is similar to mental filtering. In this type, instead of just ignoring or invalidating the good things happening to the person, she actively rejects them. People with this distortion view good things in life as flukes.

Sheens got an award for handling a crisis situation well at the office. Instead of being proud and happy, Sheens thinks that anyone in that position would have done well in such a situation.

Ravi lost ten kgs in a span of six months with a lot of hard work and determination. When his friends appreciated him for this, he just shrugs their compliment and says 'you guys are just being nice to me'.

Discounting the positives takes away the joy from life and makes one feel inadequate and unrewarded.

5. Jumping To Conclusions:
Mind reading:

Person with mind reading interprets things negatively and concludes based on their faulty assumptions. There would be no evidence for either their assumptions or conclusions.

Rohan comes home from work with a serious face. Sonali, his wife, thinks that Rohan is angry with her. Instead of asking him how his day/what happened, she chooses to avoid talking to him.

Fortune telling:

People with this type of distortion predict that things will go wrong to avoid doing something difficult.

Sharan kept telling his colleagues that his boss would scold him again and does not want to attend the meeting. Sharan has a difficulty in handling tough conversations and hence looks for opportunities to miss such meetings.

6. Magnification Or Minimization

This is also called the binocular effect on thinking. A person may either enlarge (magnify) the problems or shortcomings or ignore (minimise) the positives in oneself.

While coming back from work Joel's car met with an accident with a bike. Luckily, there was no major injuries to the biker. It was turning dark and no street lights on the road. As Joel was driving on his side of the road, a biker suddenly came sliding from the other side of the road and fell near the wheels of Joel's car. Joel, a careful driver applied breaks and stopped the car. He got out and checked on the biker's safety and attended to him. People who saw the accident mentioned that it was neither Joel's nor biker's fault. A tempo hit the biker and he lost control.

Joel kept replaying the scene in his mind multiple times and told himself he was careless while driving. He ignored the fact that applying a timely brake had saved the biker from major injuries.

What Can We Do About Cognitive Distortion?
Change Roles:
If you are Joel, imagine your best friend to be in Joel's situation. Ask yourself what you would have told your best friend when he has faulty thinking?

Challenge your thoughts:
In case of Sonali, ask her where is the evidence that her husband is angry on her.

Be mindful about your thoughts and unusual physical symptoms:

If you are feeling uncomfortable about something, pay attention to your thoughts. Write down what is running in your mind. Pay attention to your body. Identify if there is any muscle tension, sweating, racing heartbeat and so on. Ask yourself when did those symptoms start and note them down. You can use the below template to write down your thoughts.

Describe the uncomfortable situation	What were the thoughts in your mind then?	What was the emotion? Are there any unusual physical symptoms?
		Emotions: Unusual physical symptoms:

Cognitive Behavioural Therapy (CBT) helps to understand, identify and deal with faulty thinking.

7. Emotional Reasoning:

People with this type of negative thinking may be seeing the facts through their feeling's lens. This makes the reality distorted. People with anxiety and panic disorder use this lens more often than others.

Sara is a team lead and responsible for the overall delivery of the project. She is a workaholic, works long hours and most of the weekends to ensure that the deadline is met. When she foresees delivery slippage, Sara feels guilty. She thinks she must have missed something or done something wrong which is leading to delivery slippage and ends up working more due to guilt. In reality, delivery slippage might have happened due to unplanned leaves of her team members, unforeseen technical challenges consuming more time, additional ad hoc work requests in between. As Sara is wearing a lens of her feelings, she is unable to rationalise the cause for the slippage.

8. Should Statements:

People with this type of distortion, criticises self or other people with 'should' or 'should nots. 'Musts', 'Have tos' and 'Ought's' give a similar effect. This type of thinking creates fear or worry to the individual. It also creates unnecessary pressure on the person.

Suhas is good at studies. As the exams near, he starts thinking I should be the topper. As this thought intensifies, Suhas starts worrying what if he does not be the topper. It creates a lot of pressure for him. The pressure and worries do not allow him to focus on his studies.

9. Labelling:

People with this distortion label themselves or others in a negative way based on a single event or few incidents. This can lead to misunderstanding people, underestimate self or others or perceive things wrongly leading to problems between people.

Akshay sees Emma having an argument on the road with a fellow biker. He judges Emma as an aggressive person based on one incident.

Raka is a class teacher for Goel. Goel scores very less in the first test in all the subjects as his parents are going through a divorce. Raka labels Goel as a poor student.

10. Personalization And Blame:

In this type of negative thinking pattern, a person blames self or others solely for a situation when multiple factors are involved.

Shika blames herself when her husband falls sick due to food poisoning. She keeps telling as she missed cooking that day, her husband had to eat outside and fell sick. In reality, her husband is allergic to chats and he was tempted to eat chats and gave in.

What Can We Do About Cognitive Distortion?

Separate your thoughts from emotions:

Feelings are different from thoughts. We often mistake our thoughts for feelings. Ask a student who has scored less marks in an exam, 'How are you feeling after seeing the result?'. Most probably he may answer 'I should have put more effort. Why did I waste my time playing? And so on. While these are thoughts, the student may be going through the emotions of anxiety and guilt.

When you feel uncomfortable, name the emotion. Sara feels uncomfortable as soon as she foresees a delivery slippage. Sara can ask a question to herself, 'How am I feeling as I foresee a delivery slippage? Guilty? What makes me feel guilty? Did I really go wrong? Are there any other reasons for slippage?' These questions will help Sara to remove the emotional lens and see the reality

Reframing thoughts:

Reframing thoughts is observing the unhelpful thoughts in the mind and changing them into helpful thoughts.

In the case of Suhas, replace the thought 'I should become a topper' to 'It is nice to be a topper/I want to become a topper. What can I do to reach there?'

In the case of Shika, the thought, 'Because I missed cooking, he fell sick' leads to guilt. Instead, Shika can reframe it into, 'Next time I need to remind him to be careful while eating outside.'

In a nutshell, recognizing and understanding cognitive distortions can help us to deal with negative patterns of thinking and avoid psychological damage and relationship issues they cause.

Have you noticed negative thinking in yourself? What do you want to do about it?

While the techniques given will help you to a certain extent to deal with cognitive distortion, it is better to see a therapist if the distortion is severe and interfering in day today life.

17
In The Lap Of Anxiety

Rukma was getting ready for the office. She was already running late and Janani's repeated calls irritated her. While she kept declining the calls, she also wondered if there was any emergency for Janani to reach her. She booked the taxi and dialled Janani's number as she waited for the taxi to arrive. Janani received the call after four rings.

'Hey Ruks, congratulations my dear! I am very happy as well as mad at you. Mad at you because I got to know the news from someone else. It was unbelievable at first when I heard the news but later, I was so happy and excited for you', Rukma recognized the excitement and complaint in Jajani's tone. She replied to Janani as she sat in the taxi, 'Thank you Janani. Sorry, I wanted to call you but the work has been so hectic you know. Anyways, I am fulfilling your dream?'. Rukma laughed as she said this.

'See, how nice it would have been if you had taken this decision seven-eight years ago? You had been so rigid on your decision'. Rukma never liked this complaining tone of Janani. Though Janani was a childhood friend, Rukma never felt like sharing her views or feelings with Janani. She didn't feel Janani understood her feelings. Janani had the habit of advising others. Rukma felt Janani was not empathetic. She refrained from sharing her feelings because of Janani's nature of nagging and sarcasm. That's the reason Rukma intentionally had not shared the news of her marriage with Rohit. Rukma quickly closed the discussion with Janani to take a nap on the way to the office.

Rukma's parents started to look for a boy after she turned 25. Rukma was well qualified and was working in a top MNC. She was a combination of beauty and brains. Rukma's parents had found many suitable boys with good family backgrounds all these years. But for some reason, Rukma didn't agree to any of them. After five-six years, Rukma's orthodox mother started pleading with her, 'If you are in love with someone, even if it is from some other caste, we will marry you to him'. As Rukma grew old, some started talking about her marital status. 'She has a lot of ego as she earns more', 'She is very stubborn, she does not listen to anyone', 'Looks like she does not want to marry 'and so on. Some people who were close to her took the liberty and used to condemn her directly. One friend said, 'Looks like you have a lot of demands, that's why no guy is saying yes to you'. A colleague commented 'You are very complicated Rukma, that's why you are not married till now'. In the last ten years, Rukma had heard many comments on this matter. She used to feel very sad when she was blamed for not being married yet.

Either people gave advice or scolded her. They did not make an effort to understand if she was facing any challenge or how she felt overall about meeting guys. Her parents did make an attempt once or twice. As those conversations turned to arguments and ended with Rukma getting angry and crying, her parents stopped questioning her decisions.

In reality, Rukma neither was in love with anyone nor had decided not to marry. In fact, she could not understand why she was unable to decide upon a suitable match. It was a puzzle to her. She knew she didn't have valid reasons to say no to some of the guys. When she thought of discussing her challenge with anyone, she would hear 'You are overthinking Rukma. Your parents would have checked upon the guy and the family. Just say yes', 'The guy is earning well and not staying with parents. What else do you want?' or so on. Others would extrapolate their experience to her future and say, 'Whomever you marry, it is the same experience! take care of the husband, kids and home. So why are you delaying?'. Rukma felt like not opening up to anyone because they were more interested in advising than listening. She felt sad about her struggle to decide on marriage. She felt guilty of putting her parents through a tough ride. She felt helpless. No one could even make out she was going through all these feelings.

Six months ago, she bumped into her childhood friend Rashmi in a mall. Both the friends were very happy to reconnect with each other. They took a break from work that day and decided to spend their day at Rashmi's home. They enjoyed sharing life's highlights from the last fifteen years. As they were discussing, Rukma mentioned how she has been very successful in her career but her challenge with deciding upon marriage. Rashmi was a good listener in her childhood too. She was very empathetic. This always gave a comfort for Rukma to confide easily with Rashmi. Now Rashmi is a psychologist too. Rashmi encouraged Rukma to talk about her thoughts around marriage. She asked how Rukma feels when she is about to meet a prospective groom.

For one of Rashmi's questions, Rukma said, 'It is very easy for me to meet and talk with any guy. All the trouble starts when I start thinking about 'should I marry him'.

'What's that trouble you face?' Rashmi asked gently.

Rukma's voice dipped as she spoke, 'I don't know Rashmi. Probably I get scared of thinking about getting married. I lock myself in a room and I sleep off'.

'So, when you start thinking about deciding to get married, you ger scared?' Rashmi repeated her statement.

'I think so. I feel short of breath. My heart beat increases'.

'Do you also sweat?' Rashmi enquired.

'Sometimes yes. As soon as I decide to say no to the guy, all these symptoms vanish', said Rukma with a sigh.

'Maybe you are experiencing anxiety. Increases in heartbeat, shortness of breath, sweating are few physical symptoms of anxiety. This may be an indication of mental health issues. But, before we conclude it is something to do with mental health, consult a doctor to rule out any physical issues. Rashmi patted her back gently.

'What? Is this anxiety? I never realised that these symptoms should be discussed with a doctor'. Tears rolled out of Rukma's eyes.

'I am there with you. Do not worry about this. Even if it is anxiety, there are different therapies which help to deal with it. We can take the help of medicines as well if just the therapies do not work'.

'For some reason Rashmi, these symptoms are all very uncomfortable to me. These symptoms appear even in other situations. As I recall, I have been avoiding the situations which cause these symptoms', Rukma shared candidly.

'Good Rukku, this awareness itself is a first step towards the therapy'.

'Rashmi, will you help me?' Rukma held her hand.

'Of course, Rukku, we will start the therapy this week itself. Meet me at the clinic the day after'.

Rashmi assessed Rukma's issue as an anxiety problem. Rukma took counselling with Cognitive Behaviour therapy and Mindfulness for six months. When she met Rohith as marriage prospect, she shared about her anxiety issue and how it has been an obstacle to decide on marriage. Rohith was empathetic and supported her to continue the therapy. All this resulted in Rukma saying yes to Rohith and their wedding was decided.

Rukma woke up with the sound of her phone ringing. She smiled looking at the mobile 'Rohith calling', and received the call.

18

The Scary Pony Ride

'You can't stop the waves, but you can learn to surf.'

- Jon Kabat-Zinn

Anxiety is an emotion which everyone experiences one or the other time. It is neither good nor bad by itself. The good or bad is based on the situations where it appears. Here is a personal story about anxiety and ways of dealing with it.

It was in my bucket list to visit Kashmir for a long time. Hearing the news about the terrorist attacks in Kashmir from the media, I was always anxious to plan a trip to this place.

When my husband expressed his desire to see the snow in Kashmir, I had to make up my mind to overcome anxiety about visiting this place and that is how this trip happened.

Once we decided to travel to Kashmir, I started following the news about it and updates on situations there. I also started talking to people who had visited Kashmir recently. We found a good travel agent who had experience in conducting tours in this place. With all these efforts, I got confidence that the tourist places in Kashmir are safe and the sensitive areas in Kashmir are at a distance of 200-250 kms away from these places. That gave me a lot of relief.

Good start is half done. I had conquered my fear to an extent to start the journey. When we landed in Srinagar airport, seeing the CRPF (Central Reserve Police Force), a shrill nervousness passed through my body. As we travelled to our houseboat in Dal Lake, we could see the CRPF here and there with big guns and rifles. My mind started generating thoughts of fear. I was getting thoughts like, 'O my god, there are so many police forces here. This place is not safe'. This was repeating in my mind. After some time, I realised that CRPF is there to ensure safety. I should feel safe because of their presence and not panic with fear. This change in perspective helped in reducing my fear. Within one day, my mind got familiar with seeing the CRPF force and got habituated with it.

First day, we enjoyed the Dal Lake and Shikara ride. On the second day, we travelled to Pahalgam to see the beautiful valleys. A view point called 'Mini Switzerland' was on our list. The only way to reach this place from the base point was on Pony (Pony is a breed of horse which is smaller in size). When I heard that we had to go on a Pony, I started to worry. My earlier experience of horse riding was not that pleasant. It was so difficult for me to get on and off the horse because of my height. I had pulled my muscles and had suffered with pain for 2-3 days. My worrisome thoughts kicked in again. 'What if I face issues getting on the horse? What if I fall down while getting down?' I started getting these negative thoughts which increased my anxiety. Also, I was scared of the terrain. I had heard stories about 'pony rides' where the pony walks on the edge of the cliff. The experiences I had heard were very scary. With a sceptical mind, I sat in the car which drove towards Mini Switzerland. Around that time, I got a call from my brother. He was checking on us and our itinerary. When I told about the pony ride, he immediately mentioned that the pony is not as tall as the horse. He had witnessed my horse experience earlier and gave me confidence that I would be able to get on the pony easily. That reduced half of my anxiety. We reached the base and started talking to the pony guys. I asked a pony guy about the terrain. Sensing my anxiety, he said that the route is not steep. With that, my anxiety further came down and I was kind of okay to explore the pony ride.

I could get on a pony without much hassle. Pony started walking. Caretaker of the Pony, the Pony Wala was also with us, walking along with the Pony. The terrain was a mix of plain and road. I was so happy and thought that unnecessarily I was scared so much. Within a few minutes, we reached a terrain that was slushy and rocky. My anxiety was back. Pony slipped twice and my heart skipped a beat. It was an uphill journey initially. Pony Wala started giving me instructions on how to have a balance on the pony. He asked us to lean forward when it was uphill and lean backward down the hill.

Initially it was difficult for me to follow his instructions. As I paid attention to him and started to follow the instructions, I was more confident to have the balance. By the time I felt I got a hold on the pony, we reached a terrain where there was a steep valley on one side, and a mountain on the other side. Pony had its own whims and fancies. It started to walk on the edge of the valley. I got very scared and started telling the Pony Wala to ask the pony to walk on the other side.

Pony Wala laughed and told me, 'Madam, this is a regular route to pony. Trust the pony and you will be safe'. I was so scared to look at the valley. My heart beat increased along with my anxiety. My thoughts raced with high-speed generating all possible negative outcomes like, 'It is so steep. What if I fall and break my leg?', 'What if I lose balance and the pony drags me on the floor?', 'What if I fall and hit my head on a rock?'. Within 10 minutes I could hear my own heart beat as it had become faster and louder.

As my thoughts became unbearable, I told myself that I need to take control of my thoughts and the discomforts in my body. I had no choice because I could not get down and walk in that terrain. That needed a knack I didn't have. My rational mind started telling me to apply CBT(Cognitive Behavioural Therapy) and other techniques to calm down my nervous system. Slowly, I started to do a 'candle breathing'* exercise. Within 5 minutes of continuous candle breathing, my heart beat slowed down. I started challenging my thoughts as I saw people who were returning from the trip on pony. 'What is the chance of me falling down?', 'How many people have fallen down the pony today?', 'There were so many people going and coming on the pony. Did I see anyone falling down?' Asking these questions and answering them helped me to bring a perspective on reality. I had not seen anyone fall down or even heard anyone falling down the pony that day. If there were a lot of falls and injuries due to the pony ride, it would have been banned. Thinking rationally helped me to isolate the perceived threats from real threats. I also realised there was a risk with pony rides. But that could be mitigated with the right knowledge, trusting the horse and following the Pony Wala's instructions.

While I was dealing with my anxiety through thoughts, Pony had its own way. It used to go off the trail or used to start running sometimes. My anxiety used to increase and my negative thoughts used to race. I started reframing my negative thoughts to positive ones. I started telling myself loudly in a rhythmic way, 'Trust the horse and lean back. Horse knows the job well' while going downhill and 'Trust the horse and lean forward. Horse knows the job well' while going uphill. Telling myself to trust the horse and keeping the right posture on the pony further reduced my anxiety and slowly I started to relax. Once I started to relax, I was able to enjoy the beautiful scenery around me. I continued with reframing my thoughts loudly and rhythmically (like chanting a mantra) and occasionally did candle breathing when my anxiety spiked.

Mini Switzerland was indeed beautiful. The way back on the Pony was much more enjoyable as I was able to relax. When we finished that trip, I was very happy with myself dealing with anxiety successfully.

Finally, the Kashmir trip was successful. We came back safely with many cherishable moments.

In a nutshell, anxiety can be managed with the right tools. Here are some pointers to manage your anxiety.

1. Knowledge is power. Knowledge from the right sources about the thing which causes anxiety helps to reduce the worries.

2. Exposing oneself to the fearing object (though it creates discomfort initially) helps in reducing the anxiety.

3. Asking questions and clearing your doubts helps to get a realistic picture.

4. In some cases, anxiety can be triggered due to lack of skill about dealing with a thing. Recognizing and building skills is crucial.

5. Practice, practice, practice. It brings down anxiety.

6. Anxiety is a perceived threat. That means it is not a real problem or the problem is not immediate. Recognize whether the anxiety is stemming from a real issue or perceived one. Real issues need to be solved while anxiety needs to be dealt with.

7. Anxiety means the human body goes to fight or flight mode triggered from the autonomous nervous system (ANS)). Candle breathing and chanting helps the ANS calm down and get out of Fight or Flight response.

8. Anxiety manifests as thoughts too. CBT helps to deal with it.

9. Share your anxiety with someone you trust.

Anxiety can be managed to a greater extent with tested techniques mentioned in this story. You can't stop the waves. But you can learn to surf. Find a professional who can teach you to surf!

19

Fight, Flight Or Freeze - Whats Behind This?

Have you experienced any situation when you acted before even thinking when encountered with danger? Have you wondered how someone managed a dangerous situation and escaped safely? Did you know that dangerous situations can switch off the thinking part of the brain? Sounds interesting? Read ahead.

'A father and son are taking a relaxed stroll on the footpath of a road. There are quite a few people around who have come out for the walk. Father is listening to his seven-year-old boy talking about his school. They are enjoying their conversation. Suddenly a biker comes very fast from behind, into the footpath. He applies a sudden brake and falls down. The biker was so close that both father and son screamed, and the boy jumps on to the father as the father grabs him up. Boy starts crying loudly, his body shivering. His heart started beating faster. Father is sweating and grinding his teeth. He starts shouting and scolding the biker on top of his voice. All these things happen very quickly and simultaneously, within a few seconds.

'A man is returning from his office by bus. He is tired after hectic work. He gets off the bus and starts walking. As he is walking in the small gullies towards his house, he hears the dogs barking faintly. The barking sound grows louder and louder. When he looks in the direction from which the sound is coming, he sees four dogs running towards him. Immediately, before he could think, he started running fast, away from the dogs. Dogs chase him for a few metres. Man is sweating profusely and his heart is beating faster. He runs to his home. From hearing the dogs bark to running home happens within a fraction of seconds.

'A mother is playing with her two daughters inside the compound of her house. The elder one who is eight years old is playing hide and seek with her two-year-old sister. They are joined by the elder daughter's friend. Once the friend arrives, the older one starts playing with her friend. Mother continued to engage the younger one. Suddenly, the mother hears the elder daughter scream. Mother turns and sees that the elder one has fallen from the compound and is crying. Mother rushes to attend her. She consoles the daughter and turns to see the younger one, but the younger one is not around. The gate is open and mother runs to see where the younger one is. As she reaches the compound gate, she feels dread seeing the scene in front of her. Her feet feel cold and she becomes numb and motionless. The elder daughter panics seeing mother startled. She runs to the gate to see a passerby, running and pulling her younger sister from the road just before the neighbour's car hits her while reversing'.

Common thing in the above scenarios is that there was a real danger and a threat to life. People who were around reacted very quickly within a fraction of seconds, without even thinking, but with a goal to save a life. Some of them showed similar unusual physiological symptoms of sweating, increase in heartbeat and shivering.

Though it was a threat for life, each had their own way of reacting to these situations. While the father chose to fight, the man opted to run away. Mother froze, not being able to move. People chose different ways to react to the stressful event. When there is a threat, we react quickly before even thinking. This acute stress response to a dangerous situation is commonly called Fight / Flight / Freeze states.

F3 Response:

Fight / Flight / Freeze response is our body's in-built mechanism to react to danger. It is a natural and automatic reaction by humans (in fact even in case of animal's) when they are faced with life threats. It is driven by quick hormonal(chemical) and physiological changes that allow a person to protect themselves immediately. Body goes to these states immediately before even a human could think.

F^3, is usually triggered by anger, fear and anxiety. Fight's primary emotion is anger and Flight's is fear or anxiety. When the body feels that 'Fight or Flight' mode cannot help to deal with the danger, it goes into a 'Freeze' state. These three states can be identified by certain unusual physiological symptoms. Some of these symptoms can be common for fight and flight states. When the body senses danger, there may be change in some of the body functions which include but not limited to change in skin colour, increased heart rate or breathing, tension in muscles, dilated pupils.

Some of these common symptoms can also appear when a person is excited with an adventure or thrilling activity like bungee jumping or receiving an award and so on.

Each state can also have distinguished physiological symptoms.

Fight

On encountering a situation, if the body feels that it is a danger and believes that you can overpower the threatening object to save yourself, the body drives you to fight. The brain signals and prepares your body physically to fight. Apart from the common unusual symptoms, fight state can also trigger tight jaws, teeth grinding, clenched fist, and so on.

Flight

On encountering a situation, if the body feels that the object of danger is more powerful than your capacity to fight, but you can avoid it by running away, you will respond with flight mode. In flight mode, a surge of hormones including adrenaline boosts the stamina to run longer than you could in normal conditions. Along with common unusual symptoms like racing heartbeat, increase in breathing, a person may also feel dry mouth, sweating, constantly moving the legs / hands and so on.

Freeze

While Fight or Flight modes exhibit decisive actions, Freeze mode does not involve any decisive actions. This response happens when the body feels that neither you can fight and save yourself nor run away and avoid. Body feels that you are stuck in the place and becomes numb. This state can accompany with loud and pounding heartbeat and pale skin from the common symptoms but the body feels a sense of dread, feels stiff and cold, and the heartbeat also can decrease.

In the above examples, the father's body chose to fight while the man's body chose to escape(flight). Mother felt so helpless that her body just froze to save her from the emotional pain.

The fight / flight / freeze states can also happen when there is no real danger. Anxiety is called a perceived threat (not a real threat) and the body feels the situation as a real threat and can show similar reactions as that of danger causing physical and mental discomfort.

Ability to understand the difference between real and perceived threat, learning CBT (Cognitive Behavioural Therapy) and some techniques to deal with unusual physiological symptoms helps to deal with anxiety.

> ADRENALINE IS THE HORMONE SECRETED BY ADRENAL GLANDS THAT IS RESPONSIBLE FOR THE F3 RESPONSE.
>
> HYPOTHALAMUS AND PITUITARY GLAND OF THE BRAIN DIRECTS THE ADRENAL GLAND TO SECRET THE REQUIRED NUMBER OF HORMONES.
>
> F3 RESPONSES ARE INSTINCT BASED OR LEARNT BEHAVIOUR.

20

Emotions & Feelings

Humans are special among all the species because they have a brain which is remarkable in cognition. They can think and feel and can solve problems, create languages, customs, cultures and so on which are so diverse in nature.

Irony is that even with this super brain, we need to be trained to recognize our emotions. We feel different emotions day-in day-out. But many of us are not skilled enough to either recognize emotions or name them. Unfortunately, this basic skill is neither taught in schools nor by our parents.

You might have come across a situation like this. Your colleague coming out of a meeting with a performance appraisal letter with a sad face. On enquiring you hear that he has not got any hike. When you ask him, 'How are you feeling?' The reply could be something like 'I knew my manager would screw up my appraisal', 'What is the use of working day and night? I think it is high time to change the company'.

You call your friend as usual. You sense that she is upset and probe her. She says, 'It is the usual fight with my mother-in-law'. You hear her sob over the phone. You ask her, 'How are you feeling?'. She would pour out probably saying, 'Every time, she does the same thing. She criticises everything I do. She does not allow me to take up responsibility but complains that I don't do enough chores at home'.

In both the cases, when the other person asked what they were feeling, the answer they shared was, what they were thinking.

Feelings or emotions are often confused with the thoughts.

Emotions & Feelings

As per Oxford dictionary, feeling means 'something that you feel through the mind or through the senses. It also mentions that 'feeling is a person's emotions rather than their thoughts or ideas'.

Merriam-Websters dictionary defines emotion as 'Emotions are conscious mental reactions (such as anger or fear) subjectively experienced as strong feelings usually directed toward a specific object and typically accompanied by physiological and behavioural changes in the body'.

Now, from the definitions, it is clear that emotions/feelings and thoughts are different. Before we deep dive, let us understand if feelings and emotions are one and the same.

Emotions are natural to all humans, regardless of age, gender or culture. As per the theory by Antonio Damasio, a neuroscientist, emotions are generated in Amygdala, a part of the brain. Brain has different parts responsible for different functions. Amygdala is one of them and it is responsible for multiple functions. This is the major processing area for emotions. It also connects the emotions to other brain functions like memories, learning and senses. When Amygdala does not work properly, it generates disruptive symptoms and uncomfortable feelings. Severe disruption in amygdala functioning can lead to mental health disorders.

According to the initial theory of Paul Ekman, a psychologist from America, there are six basic emotions that the brain generates. They include, Fear, Sadness, Anger, Happiness, Surprise & Disgust. These are called universal emotions because every human being experiences these emotions. Though these basic emotions seem like a single emotion by themselves, when experienced they come with a family of different emotional states making it complex.

So, when there is an external or internal trigger, the amygdala gives a psychological reaction to these triggers generating an emotion. When Amygdala gets activated, there are some chemical processes taking place in the brain. Amygdala starts dealing with the primary emotion and in turn can further lead to other feelings. Example, in a threatening situation the amygdala creates fear first. Then to deal with fear, it creates other feelings like stress and anxiety. So, to make it simple, emotion is like a parent and feelings are like children.

A person who experiences intense fear also may feel his heart beat(palpitation) or increase in heartbeat. So, emotion can also generate physiological responses. So, feelings also include different physical states but not limited to hunger, thirst, temperature and pain.

You can also refer to the **Wheel of Emotions** to understand more about different emotions. PLUTCHIK'S WHEEL OF EMOTIONS is one of the wheels which shows eight basic emotions, their combinations and opposites. An image of the wheel and more information is easily accessible on the internet for reference.

NAVARASA (as per Natya shastra):

SRINGARA (LOVE)

HAASYA (HUMOUR)

ADBHUTA (WONDER)

VEERA (COURAGE/VALOUR)

SHAANTHA (PEACE)

KARUNA (COMPASSION)

RUDRA (ANGER/AGGRESSION)

As we understand that emotions are triggered by an external situation or an internal event (our thoughts, emotions or physical sensations), does every situation trigger the same emotion in humans?

Generally, a wedding ceremony is a happy occasion which brings happiness to the bride and groom, relatives and friends. People usually are happy and excited around wedding time either participating in it or by remembering their wedding and feel good with the happy memories.

If the bride or the groom is being married forcefully, the wedding may trigger a different emotion like anger. A person who is not married, others' wedding news or attending others' weddings may trigger sadness in them.

Emotions are reactions to a situation or the event that humans experience. The experience is based on the type of the situation and also, how one relates the situation to oneself.

We discussed the generation of the emotion. What about its end? How long will it last?

Research says that as the generation of emotion involves a chemical process, it lasts for about 90 seconds. But the emotion can be sustained with reinforcing thoughts, situations and feelings.

Emotions are like a sine wave. It has a peak and falls down. The intensity of an emotion also keeps varying.

Are Emotions Good Or Bad?

Many of us think that anger is bad. Are emotions bad?
When you feel happy seeing your child learn to walk, is that emotion bad? When someone appreciates you for your work or gesture, you feel proud. Is that a bad feeling? You may not classify the happy feeling as bad. But if you get angry you may call that emotion bad. Isn't it?

Why is anger labelled as bad? Why isn't happiness bad? Because, anger creates discomfort in us and when we are angry, we may behave in inappropriate ways. We may shout, fight or throw things in anger. Shouting, fighting and throwing things is not an emotion. They are the behaviours we show in response to anger.

Along with your friends, you witness someone hitting a pedestrian while riding a bike. The biker loses balance but tries to escape. Some of you run behind the biker to catch him. What was that emotion generated when you saw the biker hitting a pedestrian? Was that emotion good? If you guys didn't get angry by that act, would you have tried to catch the biker?

Emotions are neither good nor bad. It is a natural process which is happening in the brain, like many other processes in our body. Anger seemed bad when you shouted at someone losing your control. Anger seemed good and justified when the biker hit a pedestrian.

Emotions can be categorised as comfortable and uncomfortable emotions. Emotions which are pleasant can be called as comfortable emotions, for example Happy, Joy, Peace and Excitement. Emotions which are unpleasant in nature, anger, sadness, hurt and so on can be categorised as uncomfortable emotions.

Now we know that emotion is neither good nor bad. Even the uncomfortable emotions are not bad.

But those uncomfortable emotions can lead to bad behaviours, which we have to be mindful of and take care of.

So, after reading this article, how are you feeling? Hold on! What is the emotion right now?

21
Mental Health & Insurance Coverage

Mental health in India is still a taboo subject. The stigma attached contributes a lot with people not willing to take professional help. Other reasons for not getting treated for mental illness are lack of awareness, lack of knowledge on whom to contact or lack of mental health professionals in that region. There are people who are aware about mental illness and willing to take help. They may not take the treatment/therapy or continue with it because of lack of affordability.

This article is about understanding whether there is health insurance coverage for mental health, what is covered and how one can avail this benefit.

As per the statistics, the Indian population in 2023 was 1.43 billion and 60-70 million among them had mental illness. The common causes for not taking timely treatment were stigma attached to mental illness and the financial barriers.

'Catastrophic Health Expenditure and Poverty Impact Due to Mental Illness in India' a study published (2023) in the Journal of Health Management, emphasises the financial impact of mental healthcare and the need for financial risk protection for households with members suffering from mental illness. According to this survey. Mental health expenses are categorised as direct & indirect. Direct being the expenses of medicines, hospitalisation, treatment and therapy costs. Indirect expenses include commute or travel to the mental health centre, expenses of food, loss of productivity and loss of wages due to leaves. This survey mentions that the average monthly Out of The Pocket Expense (patient had to pay from the pocket, not from the insurance) in 2023 ranged from Rs. 2000 to Rs.5000 in India.

Survey also says that around 21% of Indian households were impoverished by healthcare payments due to mental health issues. Interestingly, other statistics around the age group of people with mental illness states that around 37% of mentally ill people are in the age range of 36 to 59 & 34% in between 15 to 35. That means, mental illness affects the prime age of a person and affects their earnings and the capacity to earn.

By 2023, IRDAI (Insurance Regulatory & Development Authority of India) had enforced insurance coverage for mental illness to all the insurance providers in India. Though the Mental Health Act came in 2017 and enforced by 2018, it was not well adopted by the insurance companies. Pandemic forced insurance companies to bring this clause of mental health cover into action.

According to this act, it is mandatory for all insurance companies to give coverage for mental illness. Most of the health insurance policies now cover mental illness ranging from hospitalisation to therapy, depending on the policy type. Points which help to be aware of the coverage and claims are as below:

- Mental health coverage includes consultations, hospitalisation, therapy, procedures and surgeries depending on the type of the policy

- All health insurance should have cover for mental illness. Coverage depends on the plan and the premium.

- Like coverage for physical illness, mental illness also has a pre-existing waiting period. Details will be mentioned in the policy.

- There is no standard list of mental illnesses that need to be covered by the insurance provider. Mental Health Act guidelines are broader in nature and each policy/provider would have mentioned the disorder and the kind of coverage (hospitalisation only, therapy included, specific names of the disorder and so on).

- Common mental disorders covered by few insurance providers are
    - Bipolar Disorder
    - Acute Depression
    - Schizophrenia
    - Obsessive Compulsive Disorder
    - Anxiety Disorders

- Hyperactivity/Attention Disorders
- Mood Disorders
- Post-Traumatic Stress Disorder

- A few policies mention a broader term psychological disorder. One needs to call the insurance company to know the exact illnesses covered.

- Therapy and counselling charges are covered mostly in policies having OPD coverage or pure OPD policies

- Therapy/Counselling charges have a cap like Rs.10,000 or 20,000 per year based on the sum assured

Some policies clearly call out what is not supported. Dementia, Alzheimer and Parkinson are in that list. You need to read the policy carefully to understand what is covered, what is not covered. Call the agent to clarify your doubts and queries before buying the policy or during the claim.

Some of the day care procedures or therapy/counselling sessions may not have cashless facilities. These can be claimed through reimbursements by submitting proper documents to the insurance provider. Check with your insurance provider and understand the scope of coverage and documents required. Talk to your doctor/therapist and inform them of the documents required for the reimbursement. This would enable you to avail the mental health cover your health insurance policy offers you.

Most of the policies have hospitalisation coverage with specific illnesses mentioned above. However, very few policies cover therapy. United Health & Star Insurance OPD plans cover the therapy charges. Aditya Birla is said to have therapy covered through their own counsellors. One needs to call up the insurance providers and confirm before buying the insurance.

India has begun a new journey in mental health and insurance. It is a long way to ensure that people get timely treatment for mental illness. Insurance can play a major role in this direction. Being aware that there is insurance cover for mental illness, how one can avail and spreading this awareness to the needy can be a small contribution from us for a larger cause.

22

Empowerment Through Emotional Intelligence

You have got an escalation about your team not delivering on time. This is the 3rd time in a row. Your boss has called for a meeting.

Your child wakes up and resists going to school. You see the pattern repeating multiple times this year. You raise your tone and the child starts crying and throwing tantrums.

Aren't such difficult situations and conversations common in our life? We wish we do not encounter such scenarios.

When you are about to go to the meeting with your boss, you may already know what your boss says. Sometimes, you may also feel, your boss could have understood you better. He could have supported you or enabled you in handling the situation.

You may feel powerless sometimes when the child starts yelling and throwing things with emotional outburst. You may feel helpless about how to handle that situation gently.

We all go through such situations and feel not equipped enough to handle the situation. Because, we are not trained enough to handle difficult conversations and situations.

We talk a lot about empowerment in the workplace. Women empowerment as a whole in all walks of our life. When we think about empowerment, the first thing that comes to our mind is getting support from outside. Someone else is giving that power or authority to you to do something. While, this is one way of empowerment, the word also means that empowerment is the process of becoming stronger and more confident, especially to control one's own life. That means empowerment can happen from within as well, not just from outside.

Expecting others or the system to empower us is okay but getting it is not completely in our control. But one can exercise what is in one's own control. And Emotional Intelligence comes very handy in empowering oneself.

Emotional Intelligence (EI), in simple words, is being aware of, able to regulate and express our emotions constructively. Emotional Intelligence can be better understood through its four domains - <u>Self Awareness, Self-Regulation, Social Awareness & Relationship Management.</u>

Many of us would be using these four domains unconsciously in our life.

Self-Awareness:

As you walk to the meeting with your boss, you may be confident or apprehensive about the talk. You may go through complex emotions of worry, guilt or regret. There could be a mind chatter about what points you want to discuss, what is the way out/solution or whose mistake is it.

As the child starts showing the same pattern of not wanting to go to school, you may get concerned or get angry. When the child starts crying and throwing tantrums, you may get upset. Your mind may start throwing thoughts like 'What is happening to the child? Why does he show resistance to go to school' or 'He is becoming stubborn day by day? Probably a lot of pampering from the family has led to this' and so on.

These emotions and thoughts come automatically and mostly unconsciously. Making this unconscious conscious is Self-Awareness. Being observant to your emotions and thoughts in difficult situations is the first step towards being emotionally intelligent.

Self-Regulation:

When you are going to meet your boss, if you are confident and have a plan to solve, that means your emotions are pleasant. Approach is constructive. If you have unpleasant emotions - anger or guilt, regret or worries, that would reflect on how you speak, what you say - that's your behaviour. Then, it is the time to tap into your Emotional Intelligence.

Child's behaviour is a trigger and you are getting angry at the child or the others in the family for his behaviour. It is time you start exploring the next domain of EI.

Our behaviours are driven by our thoughts and emotions. Self-Regulation is regulating our unhelpful emotions and thoughts to give constructive behaviour, consciously.

You can regulate your thoughts and emotions by asking these simple questions. 'Is this emotion or thought helping me?', 'What do I want now?'. This will help you not to get emotionally hijacked and regulate your emotions and thoughts towards constructive behaviour.

Social Awareness:

Now you are aware of your emotions and thoughts as you enter your boss's cabin. You look at your boss, he seems to be cheerful and relaxed. Or he looks stern and tense. You get a pulse of what your boss might be feeling.

Child is crying and throwing things. You know that child does not want to go to school and hence this behaviour.

Before you want to tell your plan or reasons about the escalation to your boss, acknowledge how your boss is feeling. Before advising the child about the importance of going to school, acknowledge that the child is dealing with some difficulty in going to school.

Social awareness is understanding and acknowledging what the other person is going through. Empathising with them, which is the way to the next domain of Emotional Intelligence.

Relationship Management:

You are down with food poisoning. You ended up eating a lot of junk in the last week and it has made you sick. You are tired. Your family members keep telling you that 'I warned you so many times not to eat junk. See what you have gotten yourself to?', 'I knew this would happen to you. When will you listen to me!' and so on?

You are already sick and suffering. You may even be feeling guilty or angry at yourself. On top of it, you have to listen to the nagging from your family. Do you feel understood by your family? Do you feel like listening to their advice at that moment? No right?

Expressing our emotions, sharing what we really feel with our loved ones is very important in Relationship Management. In the above scenario, if your family members told you, ''It feels bad to see you suffering so much', 'Is it hurting you very badly? What can I do to reduce that pain?'', how do you feel? Do you feel understood now? Do you also understand that your family members are doing things for you out of love and care?

When they nagged you, the reason is that they are concerned about you. When they scold you about eating junk food, they are feeling bad that you are suffering. But they are unable to express this appropriately.

Sharing how you feel in a situation and asking the other person about their emotions and thoughts help to build good relationships. Telling your boss, you are also feeling upset about the escalation and sharing your thoughts helps him to understand you better. Asking him his views on it makes both of you feel you are together as a team to solve it.

Telling the child that there should be something about school which is not okay for the child and hence he does not want to go to school. Telling the child, you are concerned about the child and you want to help him makes him feel understood. Sharing some of your childhood stories about not wanting to go to school or not wanting to do some activity encourages the child to share what he is feeling and thinking. That helps to strengthen your relationship.

Emotional Intelligence, with four domains, gives us a structure to 'make the unconscious conscious' and 'empowers us from within'. It enables us to navigate through challenges in life and helps us to move towards our goals.

We can tap the power within us towards empowerment. More power to you to tap your Emotional Intelligence.

23

Habit Of Hair Pulling

Sohan is 11 years old and in 4th grade. People notice him easily, as he has patchy spots on his head.

Abra is 14 years old. She catches others attention with her uneven layers of hair.

Sohan's parents reached out to counselling as he has been seen plucking out his hair which led to visible bald patches on the head. It started six months ago with plucking out eyelashes in the beginning and moved to eyebrows and now with hair on the head. His parents were both clueless and concerned about this behaviour and consulted a counsellor based on their family doctor's advice.

Abra's teachers alarmed her parents about the hair pulling behaviour. Abra's parents, though had noticed this behaviour since a year ago, they did not think this seriously. Abra's paternal aunt also had this issue as a teenager and they felt it is normal. But Abra's teachers insisted that she get help from a counsellor as this could lead to a bigger mental health issue later, if not addressed at an early stage.

Trichotillomania is a mental health condition which involves frequent urge to pull the hair from the scalp, eyebrows or other parts of the body. Urge is so intense that one is unable to stop.

As per the psychology dictionary by American Psychology Association, 'Trichotillomania is defined as 'a disorder characterised by the persistent pulling of hair from any part of one's body on which it grows, often with conspicuous hair loss. Feelings of increasing tension before the act and feelings of release or satisfaction on completion are common. Although traditionally considered an impulse-control disorder, trichotillomania is increasingly identified as an obsessive-compulsive condition, as categorised in DSM–5 and DSM-5-TR. It is also called 'hair-pulling disorder'.

During the counselling session, Sohan admitted that he starts feeling uneasy when he is either alone or bored. There is a strong urge to pull out his hair when this uneasiness creeps in. Once he pulls out the hair, he feels a kind of pleasure and relief.

Abra recognizes that she pulls her hair in classrooms when she is unable to understand what is being taught. She feels restless and unable to focus. Then she has the urge to pull out the hair which helps her to calm down and focus back in class.

Onset of Trichotillomania is between the ages of 10-13. Symptoms are usually plucking hair from eyelashes, eyebrows, head, beard and moustache and genital area.

There is no clear cut known causes of Trichotillomania. Studies indicate the possible causes as:

- A way to deal with anxiety and stress
- Chemical imbalance in brain
- Changes in hormone levels in puberty
- Genetic - someone in the family may have it

Trichotillomania has to be treated at an earlier stage. If not treated at an early stage, it may lead to more serious problems like obsessive compulsive disorder (OCD), Depression, Anxiety disorders, self-esteem and body image issues and so on.

During the counselling sessions, Counsellor discovered that Sohan's parents were dealing with the health issues of Sohan's younger brother. This had led to less attention to Sohan, he was spending more time alone. Sohan was an outgoing child who liked to mingle with friends and play outdoors. Sohan's family had moved to a new place where the possibility of outdoor play was less and he didn't have his age group friends to play around the new place. The change of environment, lack of attention and availability of his parents had led to boredom, stress and anxiety.

During the counselling sessions with Abra's parents, it was discovered that Trichotillomania was seen in her dad's siblings. It was also discovered that her paternal grandmother had symptoms of OCD and her father having severe anxiety issues.

Abra had challenges with focusing and hence studies. The pressure to perform by parents and competition at school put a lot of pressure on her leading to stress and anxiety. Not knowing how to deal with the anxiety in a constructive way, Abra developed hair pulling as a maladaptive coping mechanism. Abra also had started developing low self-esteem issues due to her looks associated with hair loss.

Sohan's parents were counselled about how change in environment and lack of their attention is causing emotional distress to the child. Sohan was advised to use gloves when he was alone to make the hair pulling act difficult. Counsellor and parents together worked with Sohan to plan his free time to fill with activities that he enjoyed. He was also put into a tennis class so that he can fulfil his need for physical play and some socialisation.

In four months, Sohan's habit of pulling out hair had reduced. There was more hair on his head than the patches.

In the counselling sessions, Abra was able to recognise negative thoughts which accompanied her anxiety and self-doubt. She used to get thoughts like 'I am unable to understand what the teacher is saying. I am so dumb', 'What if I scoreless marks again? I will disappoint my parents. My friends will make fun of me'.

As Abra was able to recognize unhelpful thoughts and feelings, Acceptance and Commitment Therapy (ACT) and Cognitive Behavioural Therapy (CBT) was used in the counselling. The Counsellor taught her to recognize and accept her feelings of worries and anxiety from ACT and tips to challenge her negative thoughts from CBT. She was also taught a few mindfulness techniques to increase her focus and concentration. Her parents were asked to help her with additional teaching support in the subjects where she struggled.

In a year's time, Abra's hair pulling reduced as her academic performance increased. Abra falls back to hair pulling when she undergoes intense emotional distress. She understands the pattern and meets her counsellor as and when required.

Trichotillomania can be seen in different grades, mild, moderate and severe. For some people, breaking this habit may be difficult. People with this mental health condition can reach out to a psychiatrist (doctor specialised in psychiatry) for help along with counselling. In severe cases, doctors may prescribe medicines which can help to deal with anxiety associated with hair pulling.

People with trichotillomania do not pull-out hair intentionally. The act of hair pulling is an indication of the internal struggle they go through. Unfortunately, the internal struggles are mostly unseen to the outside world. Apart from counselling and medicines, these people need understanding, empathy and support from their family and friends.

It is difficult to understand any mental health condition because of the very nature of it - it is invisible unlike physical illness.

Acknowledgements

After my third book, a non-fiction on career transformation I was planning work on my favourite genre 'Memoirs' with a tinge of humour'. Creative writing demands both time and mood. As a budding solopreneur, my professional work as a Coach & a Counsellor and running my business on my own demanded a lot of time and energy from me. With that, writing consistently became a challenge.

During that time, I met Sri. Satyesh N Bellur, a Thinker, Author and Speaker who offered me to write a mental health column for Vipra Nudi journal, which gave wings to my long-time dream to write on mental health.

I am indebted to Sri Satyesh N Bellur for providing the opportunity, support and encouragement.

My heartfelt thanks to Sri Ashok Harnahalli, former advocate general of Karnataka for initiating the Vipra Nudi journal in English with rich content on various topics and providing a platform to write.

I would like to express my sincere gratitude to the Editorial Board of Vipra Nudi for their meticulous editing and support.

I am deeply grateful to Dr. C.R. Chandrashekhar, former professor of Psychiatry, Author and Padmashree awardee for going through my manuscript, guiding and writing a foreword graciously for this book.

Special thanks to my beloved friend Padma, who whole heartedly proof read and edited the manuscript.

It is incomplete without thanking my teacher and supervisor Dr. Jini K. Gopinath, Clinical Psychologist & Chief Psychology Officer at Your Dost, who guides me through the difficult cases and empowers me with his knowledge and experience.

My love and affection to my pillars, my husband and my brother, who read the articles and shared their words of wisdom, valuable feedback and encouragement. Their steadfast support has been a constant source of strength.

My deepest gratitude to my parents for their belief in my abilities. Their constant support and encouragement have been invaluable.

Needless to say, that unconditional love from my parents-in-law has been a great source of encouragement. My sincere gratitude to them for their support.

I would like to express my sincere appreciation to Orange Books for their support throughout the publishing process.

Last but not least, my special thanks to all my readers who have been great sources of inspiration throughout my writing journey.

There are many more people who were part of this journey. My heartfelt thanks to all those who made this journey possible.

About The Author

Anitha Nadig, a passionate promoter for mental health awareness, has carved a unique path in her journey from Engineer to Psychologist and Author. Originally an Engineer with 16 years of experience in the IT industry, Anitha felt a calling to make a more meaningful impact on people's lives. This led her to pursue psychology, where she discovered her true passion and founded 'Mind Sakhya' in 2020 with a mission 'to help people make friends with their minds'.

Her journey into writing began at the tender age of 10. As a teenager, her poems were recognized through publications in state magazines and competitions. This early recognition reinforced her passion for storytelling and expression.

A bilingual author, Anitha has published three books so far, two in Kannada and one in English. Her latest work, 'A QUEST FOR A NEW CAREER PATH,' has garnered significant recognition, earning her a place among the Top 50 Most Influential Authors of 2023 by The Delhi Wire.

Beyond her writing endeavours, Anitha is also a dedicated coach and counsellor. Drawing on her expertise in psychology and her personal experiences, she helps individuals navigate their mental health challenges and achieve greater well-being.

When she's not writing or counselling, Anitha enjoys reading, travelling and exploring new cultures. Her experiences often inspire her writing, providing her with fresh perspectives and unique storytelling opportunities.

www.ingramcontent.com/pod-product-compliance
Lightning Source LLC
LaVergne TN
LVHW041949070526
838199LV00051BA/2961